The Ketogenic Diet

3 books in 1:
The Ketogenic Diet Explained
The Clever Ketogenic Meal Plan
The Complete Ketogenic Cookbook

Table of Contents for The Ketogenic Diet Explained

Table of Contents for The Clever Ketogenic Meal Plan

Table of Contents for The Complete Ketogenic Cookbook

THE KETOGENIC DIET EXPLAINED

Everything You Need To Know About The Keto Diet Explained In An Easy To Understand Way

Charlotte Melhoff

Introduction

I would like to thank and congratulate you on your decision to purchase this book, *"The Ketogenic Diet Explained."* I have written this book as a guide for anyone who wants to gain a deeper understanding of the fundamental aspects of the Ketogenic diet.

One of the biggest problems that most people face when seeking information about the Ketogenic diet is getting information that is reliable, accurate, and well-explained. It is difficult to find a book that explains to you the basics of a Ketogenic diet without leaving gaps in the information provided. This is why most people are confused by the Ketogenic diet and end up believing all the negative misconceptions about it.

That is where this book draws the line. This book focuses on explaining the key concepts that you need to know to get started on a Ketogenic diet. A lot of care has been taken to make sure that every topic is covered as extensively as possible without being too technical for the reader to understand. The language has been simplified and complex theories have been broken down in a clear manner.

I have taken the time to provide technical and scientific evidence to back up many of the concepts presented here. You will find links that will lead you to studies conducted by qualified researchers who have studied the Ketogenic diet for decades. These are not my personal opinions that you have been presented here. This is credible content that is backed by science.

I have endeavoured to take you through the book in a sequential manner. You will start with the basics and then dive gradually deeper into the more complex concepts. Like I said before, everything is explained clearly so that you don't miss any crucial steps.

You will learn about how the Ketogenic diet changes the way your body works and makes you more efficient in energy production. You will discover what ketone bodies are and how they are proving to be the next big thing in research and development. You will also gain a deeper insight into how ketosis can make you stronger, faster, leaner, and more mentally focused than ever.

The Ketogenic diet offers many different benefits, some of which most people are totally unaware of. Whether it is weight loss, enhanced athletic performance, treating diabetes and cancer, or just gaining mental clarity, I can promise you that this book has what you need to achieve any of your health and fitness goals.

So, what are you waiting for? You have finally found a book that explains the Ketogenic diet in a way that is easy to follow and understand. There's no need to struggle with reading one blog after another trying to figure it all out. Everything you need to know is right here in this book!

Are you ready? Let's go!

Chapter One: Understanding the Ketogenic Diet

In this chapter, you will learn about the fundamental aspects of the Ketogenic diet. You will gain an in-depth understanding of what the Ketogenic diet is, how it works, and the different types of Ketogenic diets.

What is the Ketogenic Diet?

There are many ways of defining the Ketogenic diet. However, all the explanations of the Ketogenic diet share one common aspect: a significant reduction in your carbohydrate consumption. That is what *technically* defines the Ketogenic diet. In most cases, you will find the Ketogenic diet recommends that you get about 90 percent of your calories from fats, with the remaining 10 percent being split between proteins and carbs.

The Ketogenic diet: More fats and fewer carbs and proteins

In order to get a holistic understanding of the Ketogenic diet, we need to expand our view and get a broader definition. Let's look at what some of the published studies say about the Ketogenic diet:

- It is the consumption of fewer than 50 grams of carbohydrates daily, with 90 percent of your total daily calorie intake being in form of dietary fat (Paoli et al., 2013).

- It is the consumption of fewer than 50 grams of carbohydrates every day, regardless of your total daily calorie intake. Your fat and protein intake don't matter (Westman et al., 2003).

- It is a high-fat, low protein, and low carbohydrate diet (Freeman, 1998).

- It is a diet consisting of four times more fat than carbohydrates, with a regulated amount of protein, so that 90 percent of your calories come from dietary fat (Swink et al., 1977).

- It is a diet where 10 percent of your total daily calories are derived from carbohydrates (Accurso et al., 2008).

As you can see, all these studies are pointing to a drastic reduction in your carbohydrate intake. Though the fat and protein to be consumed may vary from study to study, it is generally recommended that you maintain a high consumption of fats with moderate protein. Therefore, it is only prudent that we take our eyes off the ratio of macronutrients and instead look at the overall goal of the Ketogenic diet.

For this reason, we should define the Ketogenic diet as a diet where the carbohydrates and proteins are in such low quantities that the body is forced to rely on fats as the *primary fuel source*. It is important to note that the carbohydrates we are talking about here are digestible (non-fibre) carbohydrates. Later, you will learn more about why it is important to

10

make this distinction, but for now, let's talk about why you shouldn't focus so much on the specific amounts of macronutrients.

Let's say that you have two individuals. One is a heavyweight boxer who consumes about 4500 calories every day, while the other is an office worker who takes in about 2600 calories daily. If they both decide to go on the Ketogenic diet and follow the general recommendation that 5 to 10 percent of your calories must be carbohydrates, the boxer will be eating 56 - 112 grams daily while the office worker will be taking in 32 – 65 grams every day (4 calories are approximately 1 gram).

You can already see that the upper limit (112 and 65 grams respectively) for both people is too high to enable fat to be the primary fuel source. In other words, though most definitions focus solely on the exact macronutrient ratios, it is also important to consider the individual's activity level, gender, body composition, and total calorie intake.

If you are just starting out with the Ketogenic diet, setting specific macronutrient goals using the above definitions will help you. However, keep in mind the underlying reason why you are doing so. Do you want to lose weight, boost your athletic performance, or use it as a therapeutic approach? Your goal should determine the macro-nutritional ratios that you adopt in your diet.

When it comes to the Ketogenic diet, do not assume that it is one of those one-size-fits-all approaches. There are many variables to consider. This is why the focus should be on bringing your carbohydrate and protein consumption low enough to force your body to rely on fats for energy production.

But why is it important to reduce carbs and proteins in your diet and increase your fat intake? Well, it's all about achieving a state known as *ketosis* and producing *ketone bodies*. In order to understand these terms, you first have to know how the Ketogenic diet works.

How the Ketogenic Diet Works

The human diet is made up of three macronutrients – carbohydrates, proteins, and fats. In an ideal world, you should be consuming these macronutrients in the right ratios so that you can stay as healthy and lean as possible. Of course, this will depend on several external factors such as age, health goals, body composition, etc.

However, for a long time now, our modern (or Western) diet has consisted of large quantities of carbohydrates with moderate proteins and very little fat. The body breaks down the carbohydrates into the simplest molecule possible, which is glucose. When glucose molecules enter your bloodstream, your pancreas automatically releases a hormone known as insulin. Insulin has two roles to play here. It can either transport the glucose molecules to the body tissues that need energy at that specific time, or it will store the excess glucose in the form of glycogen in the liver in case the body has no immediate need for glucose. The body prefers glucose because it is a simple molecule that is very easily absorbed into the bloodstream.

That is why whenever you feel hungry you immediately crave for a snack that is filled with sugar. Foods such as cakes, cookies, and pies are all carb-heavy foods.

When hunger pangs strike, the "normal" thing is to grab a sugary snack

They contain a lot of carbohydrates that can be broken down into blood glucose. Your body will take the glucose it needs from these foods and then store the excess in the form of fatty tissue. Of course, since glucose is used up so quickly, you will soon start feeling hungry again, grab another cookie, and continue the cycle. This is why our society today is facing a health crisis with diseases such as obesity, cardiovascular ailments, and even cancer.

However, the Ketogenic diet recommends that you should slash your carbohydrate consumption and instead eat a lot of fats. Why is this necessary? The simple reason is that your body needs to go into ketosis. Ketosis is a metabolic condition where your body stops utilizing glucose and instead breaks down fats within the body to generate energy. Think of it as a form of fasting, except in this case, you are still eating food. It is important to note that ketosis cannot occur unless there is a reduction in blood glucose and glycogen levels. So how does this work exactly?

When you reduce your carbohydrate intake, your body experiences a corresponding reduction in energy. You may feel weak and probably get a bit cranky. This is because your body is no longer getting enough blood glucose to generate energy. So now your body needs to find an alternative energy source. So, what is the next best option? As we already mentioned before, there is the glycogen stored in your liver. Unfortunately, on a Ketogenic diet, your glycogen reserves can only last approximately 48 hours (Adam Perrot et al., 2006).

So now that your blood glucose and glycogen levels are depleted, what next? Since there are only two other macronutrients left – proteins and fats – your body must find a way to convert one of these into energy. Protein makes a great source of energy, but the problem is that it is stored in the form of muscle. If your body starts breaking down muscle to produce energy, you will end up too weak to engage in any physical activities. Think of this from a prehistoric perspective. If your muscles have been depleted and a predator suddenly shows up, you wouldn't be able to run away or even fight.

13

So, the only viable option is fats. Your body is forced to break down fats into ketone bodies (also referred to as ketones). This is where we get the terms Ketogenic and ketosis. Ketones are the result of the partial breakdown of fatty acids in the liver, and these ketones are then used as a source of energy.

Most people think of ketosis as an unnatural condition, but nothing could be farther from the truth. You regularly undergo ketosis without even realizing it. If you eat at seven p.m. and then take your next meal at nine a.m. the next morning, your body would be in a minor state of ketosis because you would have been fasting for at least 14 hours. The challenge that we have is that we are constantly snacking on carbohydrates, and therefore, our bodies never get the chance to experience steady ketosis.

We shall go deeper into the ketosis process and ketone bodies in Chapter 2, but for now, let's learn about the different categories of Ketogenic diets.

Categories of Ketogenic Diet

Earlier in the chapter, we learned that defining a Ketogenic diet should be more about knowing your goals rather than just becoming obsessed with the exact percentages of carbs, protein, and fats. You also learned that it is not a one-size-fits-all approach.

The reason for this is that there are four different types of Ketogenic diets, and each one is defined according to an individual's lifestyle and goals. The Ketogenic diet can be used for losing weight, growing muscle, and healing certain diseases. Let's find out more about these types of Ketogenic diets.

1. The Standard Ketogenic Diet (SKD)

The Standard Ketogenic Diet is the one that most people start off with. It is a very simple approach that recommends you consume the least amount of carbohydrates every day. The SKD recommends about 20 to 50 grams of net carbohydrates daily, though the exact amount will depend on your personal needs. This is the best form of Ketogenic diet for people who want to lose weight.

2. The Targeted Ketogenic Diet (TKD)

The Targeted Ketogenic Diet is primarily for individuals who engage in a lot of regular physical exercise. It recommends that you eat between 25 and 50 grams of net carbs, 30 - 60 minutes prior to engaging in a strenuous workout. The carbs you consume must be easily digestible and have a high Glycemic Index (GI). Glycemic Index is simply a number that tells you how quickly your body will convert a carb into glucose. The higher the GI number, the faster the rise in blood sugar. Since the TKD is used when you need a quick energy boost for your exercise, you should go for foods that increase your blood sugar very quickly, such as bananas, potatoes, or white rice.

Since the carbs that you eat before exercising move quickly through the bloodstream, the glucose will be burned up during the workout without causing an excessive disruption to ketosis. After the workout, the TKD recommends that you eat a meal high in protein but low in fat. The reason is that too much fat after exercise will hinder absorption of nutrients and recovery of muscles. It is important to note that TKD is not recommended for everyone.

3. The Cyclic Ketogenic Diet (CKD)

This is a Ketogenic diet that requires you to alternate between days of low carb consumption with days of excessive carb intake. This kind of Ketogenic diet is preferred by athletes who want to cut fat and build lean muscle, for example, bodybuilders and wrestlers.

It involves consuming about 50 grams of carbs on Ketogenic days and then consuming around 450 - 600 grams of carbs for the next 24 to 48 hours. It is clear to see that CKD is *definitely* not recommended for the average person who just wants to stay healthy or lose weight.

4. Restricted Ketogenic Diet (RKD)

This type of diet is recommended for people who are undergoing some form of medical treatment. According to a study published in the Nutritional and Metabolism Journal, the restricted Ketogenic diet can be used to treat malignant cancers. Restricting your carbohydrate consumption to 20 to 50 grams a day causes your glycogen reserves to be depleted, and ketones are then produced as an alternative energy source.

While healthy cells will be able to utilize ketone bodies, the cancerous cells won't, and they will begin to starve to death. Other ailments that can be treated using the RKD include Parkinson's disease, depression, epilepsy, Alzheimer's, chronic fatigue syndrome, and many others.

Chapter Summary

Here are the key points of this chapter that you need to remember:

● Though there are many different ways of describing the Ketogenic diet, depending on which study you follow, the underlying factor is that it involves a significant reduction in carbohydrate consumption.

● The Ketogenic diet is a diet where carbohydrates and protein levels are so low that the body must rely on fats to produce energy.

● When carbohydrates are consumed, they are broken down into blood glucose. This triggers the release of insulin which either sends the glucose to body tissues or stores it in form of liver glycogen.

● Reduction in carbohydrate consumption triggers ketosis, which is a metabolic state where your body breaks down fats instead of carbs to generate energy.

● For ketosis to occur, blood glucose levels must be significantly reduced, and there must be a depletion of all liver glycogen reserves.

● In the Ketogenic diet, you must consume a lot of dietary fats so that your body can break the fats down into ketones. Ketones provide an alternative energy source whenever you run out of blood glucose.

● There are four types of Ketogenic diets. Each diet is specifically suited for a particular lifestyle or specific goals. They include the Standard Ketogenic Diet (for weight loss), the Targeted Ketogenic Diet (to boost athletic performance), the Cyclic Ketogenic

17

Diet (to cut fat and build muscle), and the Restricted Ketogenic Diet (for treating diseases).

In the next chapter, you will learn more about ketone bodies and how the overall ketosis process works.

Chapter Two: Understanding Ketosis

In this chapter, you will learn more about ketosis, how ketone bodies are produced, how to measure your ketone levels and learn the signs of ketosis.

Ketones

For most of our lives, we have been led to believe that we cannot survive without carbohydrates. We have been taught that carbohydrates are necessary to produce glucose as the primary source of energy.

But what we were never told is that there is an alternative source of energy that the body can use under a myriad of conditions. This energy source is much more efficient than glucose and is often ignored and underutilized. This energy source is ketones.

Ketone bodies are created when the body breaks down fats. Your body cells then use ketone bodies as fuel to perform regular functions. From a scientific point of view, ketones are a collection of organic molecules that can dissolve in water and have an extremely specific chemical structure. However, there are a few specific ketones that are produced when the body undergoes nutritional ketosis.

These are the three types of ketone bodies:

- Beta-hydroxybutyrate (BHB)

2-Hydroxybutyric acid

Chemical Structure of BHB

- Acetoacetate (AcAc)

Acetoacetate

Chemical Structure of AcAc

- Acetone

Acetone

Chemical Structure of Acetone

The above ketone bodies are referred to as *endogenous* ketones because they are naturally produced by the body. This differentiates them from another class of ketones that are made artificially and are available in ketone supplements. These are known as *exogenous* ketones. For now, we will focus primarily on endogenous ketones.

Each of the three ketone bodies above performs a unique purpose in the body and can be detected using a special technique. For example, BHB (also known as hydroxybutyric acid) is measured through a blood test. AcAc is measured in the urine using a urine strip, while acetone is detected in the breath using a breath metre.

It is important to note that at any given time during the day, your body may have a differing number of ketones in the bloodstream. As we learned before, the supply of ketones is never constant because of our habit of eating carbs every chance we get. Since glucose is always readily available, the body simply uses it for energy and leaves the fatty tissue alone. But when there is a drop in blood sugar levels (glucose is still available but in very small amounts), ketones become the primary energy source.

How to Measure Ketones

One of the biggest concerns for someone who has just started on the Ketogenic diet is whether they are doing it the right way. It can get pretty confusing trying to figure out what the optimal ketone levels should be to induce a state of ketosis.

The normal ketone level for anyone who is consuming a carbohydrate diet is 0 - 0.4 millimole per litre (mmol/L). Ketosis is generally achieved when the level of ketone bodies in the bloodstream go above 0.5 mmol/L. So, the only way to know whether there are enough ketones to be used as an alternative energy source is by measuring your ketone levels.

The ketone levels in your bloodstream are considered to provide a more precise reading than your urine or breath. However, measuring blood ketones is also the most expensive way of determining ketosis, so most people choose to measure their breath or urine ketone levels.

Another issue to consider is the unit of measurement. If the device you are using is graduated in milligrams per decilitre (mg/dL), you will have to divide that reading by 10.2 to convert it into mmol/L.

There are three techniques for measuring ketone bodies:

1. Blood Ketone Metres

This device is similar to what you use when you want to measure your blood glucose levels. The blood ketone metre comes with a ketone measuring strip. You simply attach the strip to the metre, prick your finger, and then use the measuring strip to soak up a drop of your blood.

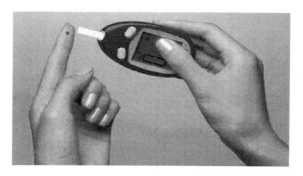

One drop of blood is all it takes to get a ketone reading

The ketone metre will then give you a reading for your BHB level. Your ketone levels should be anywhere between 0.5-7 mmol/L. Each measuring strip can cost as much as $4.

2. Urine Strips

These are cheap strips that give you a fast and easy way to detect you Acetoacetate (AcAc) levels. All you need to do is dip the strip into some urine and then wait for the colour to change according to your AcAc levels. This is a good choice for beginners.

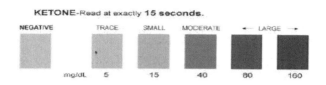

The ketone colour codes of a urine strip

However, urine strips are not as accurate as the blood ketone metre because you are depending on a colour change rather than an actual number reading. Another challenge is that urine sticks only measure the excess AcAc that is excreted rather than the actual amount available to be converted to energy.

3. Breath Ketone Metre

Unlike the first two techniques, the breath ketone metre doesn't involve strips and is reusable. You simply charge the device using a USB plug and let it warm up for a couple of minutes. Then you blow into the device continuously for 6 to 15 seconds and check your acetone reading.

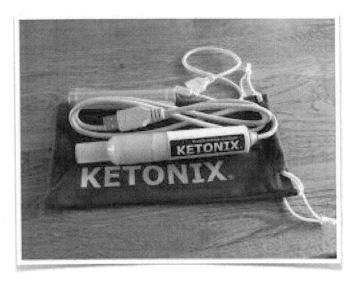

An example of a brand of breath ketone metre

One of the questions that people ask is whether it is important to know your precise ketone levels to benefit from the Ketogenic diet. While some experts claim that it is not necessary, others say that it is beneficial for beginners to do so. Remember what we learned earlier about how the Ketogenic diet is not a one-size-fits-all approach? Well, different people require different macronutrient levels to achieve ketosis.

Here is a graphical illustration of recommended ketone levels according to your goal:

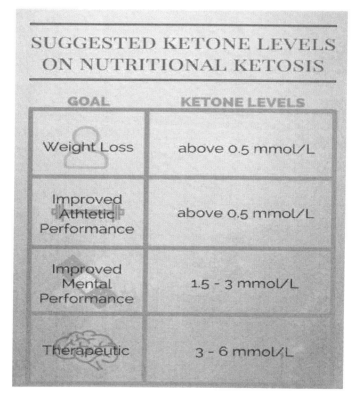

GOAL	KETONE LEVELS
Weight Loss	above 0.5 mmol/L
Improved Athletic Performance	above 0.5 mmol/L
Improved Mental Performance	1.5 - 3 mmol/L
Therapeutic	3 - 6 mmol/L

Recommended ketone levels to achieve nutritional ketosis

Therefore, measuring your ketone levels at the beginning will help you determine how much carbs and protein to eat, while also enabling you to perform random checks to see whether you are staying on track or not. However, don't let these measurements be a source of stress. Just use these techniques to help you tweak your diet to achieve your goals.

Signs of Ketosis

If you have decided to go on the Ketogenic diet, you must know the different signs and symptoms that accompany ketosis. There will be some biological adaptations that your body will undergo, including less insulin production and increased breakdown of fat.

However, these are internal indicators that you cannot physically see. So, here are some of the common positive and negative (yes, there are some not-so-positive indicators) signs of ketosis:

1. Bad Breath

This is a result of the increased acetone levels released via your breath. When you achieve full ketosis, your breath will have a fruity smell that may be somewhat embarrassing in social situations. The good thing is that it is not permanent and will stop once your body adapts to the diet.

It is recommended that you chew some sugar-free gum or brush your teeth a couple of times daily. Be very careful when buying gum. Make sure that it doesn't contain any carbs that may increase your blood sugar and lower your ketone levels.

2. Loss of Weight

In the first week of the Ketogenic diet, you will experience rapid weight loss as glycogen and water are quickly used up. After that, your body fat levels will begin to drop consistently as your body becomes a fat burner instead of a glucose burner. The Ketogenic diet helps you achieve both short and long-term weight loss.

3. Increase in Blood Ketone Levels

This is an obvious sign of ketosis. As blood sugar drops, ketone levels go up. As you progress with your Ketogenic diet, more fat will be broken down and ketones will become the main energy source. Ketone levels can be measured using specialized metres and strips, depending on the type of ketone body you want to measure. Most studies prefer to use a ketone blood metre to measure ketosis due to its accuracy. Nutritional ketosis is said to be induced when your blood ketones generate a reading of 0.5 - 3 mmol/L.

4. Increase in Ketones in Urine

Excess ketones are also released in the urine, and these can be measured using specialized measuring strips. However, the presence of ketones in urine is not a very reliable sign.

5. Suppression of Appetite

Most people tend to experience a lack of hunger when on the Ketogenic diet. According to research conducted by the University of Melbourne's Department of Medicine, the Ketogenic diet causes appetite regulation due to suppression of the ghrelin hormone. Ghrelin is the hormone that is responsible for sending hunger signals to the brain. The study showed that participants had lower concentrations of ghrelin during ketosis.

6. More Energy and Focus

During the initial stages of ketosis, you may experience some feelings of fatigue and brain fog. This effect is what makes most people quit the Ketogenic diet during the early stages. This short-term fatigue can even affect your exercise performance, but as we will learn in chapter 5, performance returns to normal after several weeks. This fatigue is simply part of the adaptation process as your body needs time to switch from utilizing glucose to burning ketones for fuel.

However, once your body adapts, you will have more energy and greater focus. Research has shown that ketones are the best source of energy for brain cells and can even be used to treat brain conditions like memory loss and concussions.

Studies show that ketone bodies can boost mitochondrial efficiency in the brain. In other words, your brain will be able to perform better on ketones than on glucose. After a while, most Ketogenic dieters tend to experience more mental clarity and enhanced brain function. The lack of carbs and stabilized blood glucose levels also contribute to this effect.

7. Digestion Problems

Since you will have to make drastic changes to the kinds of foods you eat, the initial phase of the Ketogenic diet usually involves some digestive issues. These include diarrhoea and constipation. These signs are also temporary as your body adjusts, though it is important to know which foods are causing you problems. Make sure that you get adequate low-carb vegetables that have a lot of fibre.

8. Insomnia

Most Ketogenic dieters experience some sleep problems once they cut their carbohydrate consumption. Some people wake up at night while others have problems falling asleep. However, this situation improves after a couple of weeks.

These are just some of the signs that indicate your body is undergoing ketosis. However, do not obsess over signs and symptoms because different individuals will have different symptoms. Just focus on achieving the results you want.

Chapter Summary

Here are some of the key points of the chapter that you need to remember:

- Ketone bodies provide an alternative source of energy that is more efficient than glucose.

- Endogenous ketones are those that are produced naturally in the body while exogenous ketones are manufactured and used in supplements.

- Three types of endogenous ketone bodies include beta-hydroxybutyrate (BHB), acetoacetate (AcAc), and acetone.

- BHB is detected via a blood ketone metre, AcAc is detected via a urine strip, while acetone is measured using a breath metre.

- Ketosis is achieved when ketone bodies are higher than 0.5 millimoles per litre (mmol/L).

- To convert mg/dL to mmol/L, divide the value by 10.2

- There are certain signs that indicate a state of ketosis. These include bad breath, weight loss, appetite suppression, short-term fatigue, enhanced mental focus, insomnia, and digestive issues.

In the next chapter, you will learn about the major benefits of the Ketogenic lifestyle.

Chapter Three: Benefits of the Ketogenic Diet

In this chapter, you will learn about some of the major benefits that the Ketogenic diet has to offer. Throughout the years, many studies have proven that weight management is possible with this type of nutritional approach. However, there are many other health benefits that accrue from reducing your consumption of carbohydrates.

Here are the major therapeutic benefits of the Ketogenic diet:

Weight Loss

The biggest reason why more people are becoming overweight and suffering from poor health today is that the Westernized diet promotes excessive consumption of non-fibre carbohydrates as the primary source of energy. The more carbs you eat, the more you hinder your body's ability to burn body fat.

There are many studies that have provided strong evidence to support the use of the Ketogenic diet as a weight-loss therapy. This is especially in cases that involve obese individuals. In a study published in the *Experimental and Clinical Cardiology Journal*, 83 obese patients were put on the Ketogenic diet for 24 weeks to determine whether they would experience any long-term weight loss. The 44 women and 39 men had their body mass index and body weight measured before and after the experiment.

The results after 24 weeks showed that the participants experienced a significant reduction in body mass index and weight. There were also no significant side effects as was previously thought.

Reduction in Risk of Cardiovascular Disease

There are several studies that have pointed to the beneficial effects of the Ketogenic diet in lowering cardiovascular risk factors. A few years ago, medical practitioners had doubted its effectiveness and safety compared to low-fat diets. This was because many people believed that consuming a high-fat diet would lead to weight gain and high cholesterol levels.

However, this theory has been disproven. Many recent studies show that a low-carb diet can actually lead to considerable benefits in your blood lipid profile. This means that the Ketogenic diet reduces the concentration of fat in your bloodstream.

LIPID PROFILE

	DESIRABLE	BORDERLINE	HIGH RISK
Cholesterol	<200 mg/dl	200-239 mg/dl	240 mg/dl
Triglycerides	<150 mg/dl	150-199 mg/dl	200-499 mg/dl
HDL cholesterol	60 mg/dl	35-45 mg/dl	<35 mg/dl
LDL cholesterol	60-130 mg/dl	130-159 mg/dl	160-189 mg/dl
Cholesterol/ HDL ratio	4.0	5.0	6.0

The only blood lipid that should be high is your HDL cholesterol

Your LDL cholesterol, blood glucose, and triglyceride levels are reduced while your high-density lipoprotein (HDL) levels are increased. Since LDL, triglycerides, and blood glucose levels are indicators of potential cardiovascular problems, consuming a low-carb diet will lower the risk of developing cardiovascular diseases.

Reduced Risk and Treatment of Type 2 Diabetes

The major factor that causes Type 2 diabetes is insulin resistance. But what exactly is insulin resistance and how does the Ketogenic diet help in preventing it?

The role of insulin is to activate key enzymes to store energy from carbohydrates in the form of fat. Insulin also takes blood glucose and passes it into cells so that it can be converted into energy.

When there is a reduction in carbohydrate consumption, there is also a corresponding drop in insulin production and less fat accumulation. If a healthy person (who happens to be insulin sensitive) goes on a low-carb diet, their pancreas will produce very little insulin because they don't need a lot of the hormone to transfer glucose into the cells.

However, a person who suffers from Type 2 diabetes has a problem. Type 2 diabetes develops when you consume excess carbohydrates over an extended period of time. Every time you eat carbs, blood glucose is produced, and insulin quickly moves in to transfer the glucose into the cells. At first, the cells can handle the job of absorbing and converting the blood glucose into energy.

But as you eat more carb-heavy foods over time, the cells begin to get tired of handling such a large load of blood glucose. Sooner or later, the cells refuse to respond to insulin's attempts to transfer glucose into the cells. At this point, we say that a person has become *insulin resistant*. The excess blood glucose and insulin are forced to stay in the bloodstream, and this creates a toxic condition we know as Type 2 diabetes. Another side effect will be the storage of the available blood glucose in form of fat.

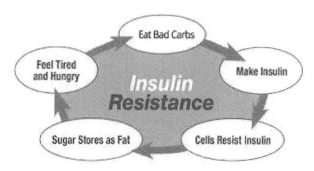

Simplified explanation of insulin resistance

Studies show that by reducing your consumption of carbohydrates, even a person who is suffering from Type 2 diabetes will experience an improvement in symptoms of insulin resistance. One study showed that individuals with Type 2 diabetes reported a reduction of insulin in the bloodstream after a few weeks of adopting the Ketogenic diet. There was also a significant loss of body fat. This proves that the Ketogenic diet can not only prevent, and treat, Type 2 diabetes.

Cancer Treatment

Cancer is one of the most devastating diseases in the world today. However, it is shocking that most medical professionals have chosen to ignore the fact that cancer has its roots in mitochondrial and metabolic dysfunction rather than abnormal DNA. Most doctors believe that cancer is caused by damaged DNA cells, but studies are showing that the cause goes much deeper than that. Cancer is simply a disease brought about by prolonged poor dietary choices that, later on, affect your DNA.

Did you know that, just like healthy cells, cancerous cells also require insulin and glucose to survive? Most cancer cells have insulin receptors and studies show that insulin can actually stimulate promotion, progression, and growth of cancerous tumours. This means that we can control cancer by denying cancerous cells access to insulin and glucose, and the best way to do this is to switch the body's primary energy source from carbs to fats.

32

On top of that, lowering your protein intake can also hinder the process through which cancer cells multiply. By adopting the Ketogenic diet, you can not only treat cancer but also prevent it. Without enough glucose, insulin, and protein, cancerous cells will simply starve to death. This shows you just how powerful a diet low in carbs and protein but rich in fats can help deal with the cancer menace.

Improved Brain Health

Research has shown that when it comes to brain health, you are better off burning fat for energy than glucose. The reason is that fat has a neuroprotective and neuro-therapeutic effect on your brain. This means that fats are able to protect the neurons in your brain and heal any damaged parts within it.

Even though fats may be unable to pass through the blood-brain barrier, ketone bodies can. In fact, ketone bodies are the only energy source that the brain has apart from glucose. Since ketones are soluble in water, they can easily cross from the bloodstream and into the brain to provide it with nourishment. Ketone bodies also help to reduce any systemic inflammation of the brain. Most people report experiencing enhanced levels of cognition and mental sharpness a few weeks after entering ketosis.

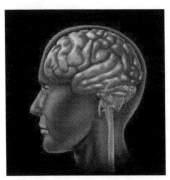

Ketosis keeps your brain healthy and alert

People who suffer from neurological diseases like Parkinson's, Alzheimer's, and ALS (amyotrophic lateral sclerosis) tend to have neurons that are insulin resistant or unable to utilize glucose efficiently. This means that their brain cells cannot get access to energy to stay alive. As a result, the neurons start dying. However, ketones do not require insulin to cross any kind of cellular membranes. Ketone bodies however, are able to enter insulin resistant cells via diffusion, and this allows them to resuscitate neurons that were previously dying and even make them thrive again.

Treating Epileptic Seizures

Epilepsy is one of the medical conditions that have relied on the Ketogenic diet as a form of treatment since the 1920's. The Ketogenic diet has a very long and effective track for treating epileptic seizures that are resistant to conventional drugs. Many studies have shown that a low carb high-fat diet can help children and adults control their seizures.

Though some medical experts are of the belief that the Ketogenic diet should be the first line of therapy for treating epileptics, most doctors choose to start with conventional medication and only resort to this diet as a last resort.

However, the evidence is very clear. Research shows that 50 percent of epileptic patients experience an improvement in seizures after being put on the Ketogenic diet. The classic Ketogenic diet (where the quantity of fat is four times higher than carbs and proteins combined) has proven to be very effective in treating epilepsy.

Nervous System and Hormonal Disorders

Switching to burning fat for energy may also benefit your nervous system and hormone regulation. Two medical conditions that show an improvement after switching to fats as the primary fuel include multiple sclerosis (MS) and poly-cystic ovarian syndrome (PCOS).

MS is an auto-immune disease that causes the myelin sheath to become damaged. The myelin sheath is the protective covering around your nerves. When this sheath is damaged, the affected person develops memory problems, loss of balance, numbness, eyesight problems, and reduced motor function. A study of MS conducted in mice revealed that the Ketogenic diet can suppress inflammation and lead to enhancement of memory, motor function, and learning.

PCOS is a disease that affects women. It increases their risk of developing diabetes, breast cancer, coronary artery syndrome, insulin resistance, and high blood pressure. PCOS produces symptoms such as obesity, lack of ovulation, hyper-insulinemia (resistance to insulin), and increased production of male hormones that cause acne and facial hair.

One study asked 11 female participants with PCOS to follow a Ketogenic diet for a period of six months. The women managed to lose 12 percent of their weight and their insulin levels dropped by about 54 percent. The levels of their sex hormones also improved significantly, with two of the women even being able to conceive in spite of having a history of infertility.

Chapter Summary

Here are the key points of the chapter that you need to remember:

- Excessive weight gain is caused by consumption of non-fibre carbohydrates. A Ketogenic diet can help obese patients lose a significant amount of weight, both short-term and long-term.

- A low-carb high-fat diet lowers the risk of developing cardiovascular diseases.

- Insulin resistance is the primary cause of Type 2 diabetes. Reducing carbohydrate consumption lowers insulin production and reduces fat accumulation, thus preventing the development of this type of diabetes.

- The root cause of cancer is mitochondrial and metabolic dysfunction. The right diet can prevent the growth and spread of tumours. By lowering your carb intake, you can deny cancerous cells access to glucose and insulin, thus starving them to death.

- Ketone bodies have a healing, protective, and nourishing effect on the brain. They resuscitate dying neurons in the brains of patients suffering from neurological diseases.

- Though the Ketogenic diet has been used to treat epilepsy since the 1920's, it has yet to receive mainstream medical approval. However, the evidence shows that patients who consume four times as much fats as carbs and proteins combined experience and improvement in seizures.

- Your body runs more efficiently when it burns fats for fuel rather than glucose. This benefits your nervous system as well as hormone regulation.

In the next chapter, you will learn how to adapt to the Ketogenic lifestyle in a safe and simple way.

Chapter Four: Adopting the Keto Lifestyle

In this chapter, you will learn about adapting to the Ketogenic lifestyle. You will learn what keto-adaptation is, the phases that you go through, and how to ensure that you eat the right foods in the right way to put you in a state of ketosis.

Understanding Keto-Adaptation

Keto-adaptation is the process in which your metabolism shifts from depending on glucose to relying mainly on fats as a source of energy. As oxidation of fats increases, your body also begins to produce ketone bodies to serve as an alternative source of fuel. Fat oxidation involves the breakdown of fats into free fatty acids. These free fatty acids are then broken down further in the liver to form ketone bodies.

The free fatty acids can be used as an energy source by almost every tissue in the body except the nervous system and brain. This is why they have to be broken down further to form ketones. The nervous system and brain need ketones to work efficiently in the absence of glucose.

This whole process of transitioning from glucose to fats and ketones does not happen overnight. Your metabolism needs some time to adjust to the new diet and energy source. You may begin to see some changes in your body within a couple of days of following the Ketogenic diet, but the adaptation process itself takes weeks.

During keto-adaptation, you will experience a delay between when you first reduce your carbohydrate consumption and having an efficient fat-burning metabolism. During this period, you will feel sick (also known as keto-flu), slow, and fatigued.

Keto-flu tends to mimic the symptoms of regular flu

It is important to keep your carb intake low during keto-adaptation otherwise your body will not adapt as it should. Most people either give up or cheat by eating more carbs, but this will interfere with ketosis and you will simply be prolonging the process.

As you will learn later in this chapter, there are steps you can take to minimize those negative initial effects of keto-adaptation. For now, let's look at why keto-adaptation is important and how carbohydrates interfere with the process.

The Self-Perpetuating Cycle

One of the first things you must realize is that the more carbs you consume, the more dependent you become on glucose as a source of energy. The problem with glucose is that it is utilized so fast by the body that it leaves you hungry again within a short time. As you eat more carbs to replenish your stocks, you delay your body's ability to adapt to fat-burning. But where and how does this cycle start?

Your body can store only a very small amount of glucose, and this is done in the form of glycogen. There are two types of glycogen in the body: muscle glycogen and liver glycogen. Your liver can only store about 100 grams of glycogen while your muscles can store about 400 grams. However, the use of muscle glycogen is restricted only to the muscle that stores the glycogen. For example, the glycogen in your bicep muscle can only be used by the tissues in your bicep. In other words, muscle glycogen cannot re-enter the bloodstream and travel somewhere else.

This means that liver glycogen is the only source that the body can use to stabilise your blood sugar and provide fuel for your brain. Remember that you only have 100 grams to work with, and this is a very small amount that cannot get you through the day. If your body has not yet adapted to making use of ketones for energy, you must find a way to replenish your liver glycogen, otherwise, you will feel mentally and physically fatigued.

TABLE 2.1   Estimated Energy Stores in Humans

Energy source	Storage site	Approximate energy (kcal)
ATP/CP*	Various tissues	5
Carbohydrate	Blood glucose	80
	Liver glycogen	400
	Muscle glycogen	1,500
Fat	Serum free fatty acids	7
	Serum triglycerides	75
	Muscle triglycerides	2,500
	Adipose tissue	80,000+
Protein	Muscle protein	30,000

*ATP/CP = adenosine triphosphate/creatine phosphate

Estimated Energy Stores in Humans

There are two ways to get more glucose into the bloodstream. Option 1 is to eat some carbs, continue being dependent on glucose, and prevent your body from utilizing alternative sources of fuel. If you do this, you will find it very difficult to adapt to ketosis and the negative side effects of the initial stages will be prolonged.

Option 2 is to allow your body to manufacture glucose from protein in a process known as *gluconeogenesis*. This process is why it is not necessary to eat carbohydrates to get glucose. The body is able to make its own glucose in small amounts from protein, much the same way that Vitamin D is manufactured naturally by exposure to sunlight.

In other words, when you feel tired and hungry, you don't need to grab a carbohydrate meal. A lot of fats, moderate protein, and very little carbs are enough to help you make it through the day. Even after your liver glycogen runs out, there's no need to worry because your body will resort to gluconeogenesis and then ketosis to provide fuel for your needs.

In fact, one of the things you will notice during keto-adaptation is that you won't feel like eating or snacking as often as you did before. You will be able to skip meals and not feel as hungry. A Ketogenic diet is able to help you naturally balance your blood sugar without becoming a slave to carbohydrates.

Phases of Keto-Adaptation

Keto-adaptation generally occurs in three stages:

1. Initial Phase

During this first phase of keto-adaptation, your body will still be dependent on liver glycogen. The initial phase is very tough for most people because, in order to break the self-perpetuating cycle that we discussed previously, you must stop eating carbohydrates. During this first phase, your liver glycogen stores will be dwindling, metabolism of fat will still be sub-optimal, and ketone production will be insignificant. It is safe to say that you will experience a lot of fatigue and brain fog during the first three days to two weeks.

Then there is the water loss. One aspect of the storage of glycogen is that it requires a lot of water. Research shows that every gram of glycogen in the body requires about 3 or 4 grams of water to be stored with it. This means that as glycogen stores are depleted, you may end up losing a maximum of 2 kilograms of water! On top of that, high insulin levels usually cause water retention in the body.

Since a low-carb diet reduces insulin levels around the body, excess water can then be excreted. Therefore, you will experience drastic weight loss within the first few weeks of the Ketogenic diet.

Initially, the weight loss will primarily be excess water

However, there is one critical thing to note here. Even though you will lose water-weight during the initial phase, this will gradually decrease, and you will soon begin to lose actual fat as keto-adaptation progresses.

2. Adjustment Phase

In this second phase, your glycogen stores will have been depleted and your body will now start making ketone bodies. Some of these ketones will be released through the urine and can be measured easily using the method described in Chapter 2. This will enable you to confirm that you have achieved the right level of carbohydrate restriction. This phase usually takes between six and eight weeks.

During this phase, ketones are freely available as an energy source, but the levels are not yet stable enough. At this point, something quite interesting happens in the brain and muscles in regards to ketone use. When the levels of ketone bodies are still low, the muscles utilise them directly as a source of fuel, but as the levels increase, the muscles suddenly utilise them less and instead switch to fat as a fuel source. The brain, on the other hand, utilises ketones according to their proportion in the bloodstream. When ketone levels are low, the brain only uses a small amount that allows it to function, but when ketone levels rise above a specific threshold, supply to the brain rapidly increases.

Now that there is enough supply of energy, the brain can be fully dependent on ketones, since there is no risk of running out of fuel. Your brain doesn't need you to eat frequently to work optimally, while your muscles now depend on fat to supply energy. This aspect of keto-adaptation is the one that athletes find quite valuable.

3. Maintenance phase

In this phase, your body has adapted to ketosis. The maintenance phase simply involves making the Ketogenic diet a lifestyle, and this may take up to a year or two of consistently keeping your carbs low. The aim here is to make it a habit and continue reaping the benefits for a long time to come.

Making Keto-Adaptation Easier

It is clear to see that the initial phase of keto-adaptation can be very difficult to handle for two specific reasons. The first reason is that there is very little glucose left and not enough ketone and fat metabolism to provide energy. Therefore, the best way to cope is to **consume a large amount of fat**. Even though your ultimate goal is to utilize body fat for energy, you must still get a lot of fat from your diet, especially during the initial phase.

The fat will provide your body with essential nutrients and fatty acids which are needed for producing energy. You should know by now that there is nothing to fear by eating a lot of dietary fats, so long as they're the right kind of fats.

Start by gradually increasing your intake of healthy fats

The second reason is that your body is losing a lot of water, sodium, and potassium at a very fast rate. This is responsible for the fatigue, headaches, and weakness. Make sure that you **consume enough sodium every day**. Take about five grams or two teaspoons of table salt daily to avert these symptoms.

Table salt will help avert fatigue and headaches during keto-adaptation

You will need to get enough potassium and magnesium to prevent loss of lean muscle, cramps, dizziness, and fatigue. Meat is a good source of these minerals, but make sure that you preserve the water if you boil your meat. Potassium and magnesium tend to dissolve when meat is boiled, so use the water to **make some broth**.

Beef broth is a great source of mineral salts

You can also **take mineral supplements** to help prevent any acute effects. It is also very important that you don't forget to drink a lot of water.

Potassium and magnesium supplements will help you adapt better to ketosis

You should also ensure that you **consume very little carbohydrates**. If you start experimenting with your carb tolerance level at this stage, you will fail to adapt to ketosis. Make sure that you know just how much carbs your food contains. Choose a very low carb intake level (about 20 grams per day) and commit to it for as long as possible until your body starts to produce ketones. Once you know how much to eat, stick to it if you want to achieve total keto-adaptation.

Tracking Your Macros

Macro is a term used to refer to macronutrients, which include fats, protein, and carbohydrates. Though it is not necessary to count your calories while on the Ketogenic diet, it is always a good idea to track your macros, especially when starting out. This is the best way to know and get used to eating the correct proportions of foods.

You will be amazed at how easy it is to go overboard with your carb consumption if you are not careful. One of the advantages of tracking your macros is that it helps you look at your ratios in terms of grams rather than percentages. For example, aiming for 90 percent fat, 5 percent protein, and 5 percent carbs looks great. However, this doesn't really paint a clear picture of exactly how much of each macro you need to consume every day.

Tracking your macros at the touch of a button

If you want to track how many carbs, proteins, and fast you are consuming every day, you can use the various mobile apps that are available. There are paid apps as well as free ones on the app store of your smartphone. A great example is MyFitnessPal.com.

Chapter Summary

Here are the key points of the chapter that you need to remember:

- Keto-adaptation is the process of shifting away from glucose to fat metabolism to produce energy.

- The brain and nervous system need ketones to work efficiently in the absence of glucose.

- Glucose is stored in form of liver glycogen (100 grams) and muscle glycogen (400 grams).

- Gluconeogenesis is the process through which protein is converted to glucose.

- There are three phases in keto-adaptation. The Initial phase involves feelings of fatigue and lasts 3 days to two weeks. The Adjustment phase involves stable ketone production and lasts six to eight weeks. The final phase, which takes about a year or more, is where you get accustomed to living a Ketogenic lifestyle.

- One significant sign of ketosis in the Initial phase is a loss of water weight. This occurs when insulin levels drop, and glycogen stores are depleted.

- To make keto-adaptation easier, consume a large amount of fat, take two teaspoons of table salt daily, drink some beef broth, take potassium and magnesium supplements, drink a lot of water, and consume 20-50 grams of carbs.

- Though tracking your calories is unnecessary, every beginner should start by tracking their macronutrients in grams.

This will tell you exactly how much you need to eat and prevent overconsumption of carbs.

In the next chapter, you will learn how to live a sustainable Ketogenic lifestyle that ensures you continue reaping the benefits for a long time.

Chapter Five: Sustaining Your Ketogenic Lifestyle

In this chapter, you will learn how to make sure that you sustain a Ketogenic diet as part of your lifestyle. You will also find a long list of foods that you need to avoid if you want to stay in a state of ketosis.

Once you have identified a Ketogenic diet as being the solution to achieving your goals, you don't want to find yourself quitting along the way. Most people who give up on a Ketogenic diet probably didn't take the appropriate steps to make sure that their actions were sustainable over the long term. This is what you will learn here.

The Sustainability of Fat

One thing that you need to know is that using fat as your energy source is much more sustainable than burning glucose. Eating carbohydrates when you are hungry never solves the problem because, within a short period of time, you will feel hungry again. This will be followed by a decrease in energy levels and your mood will also be affected.

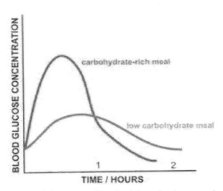

Carbohydrates cause a bigger spike in blood glucose levels compared to low-carb meals

Fat-based fuelling is more sustainable because it enables your body to access a huge store of energy without forcing you to eat frequently. But wait a minute! What about skinny people? Surely, they don't have enough fat in their bodies to fuel their needs, do they? Let's compare the levels of glycogen and fat in the bodies of people of different sizes.

The average person, regardless of size, probably has only between 1600 and 2000 calories of glycogen stored in their body. Compare this to the 30,000 – 60,000 calories of fat that a skinny person stores in their body! For a person of average build, this figure goes up to 100,000 calories of fat, and for an obese individual, it's about 200,000 calories! This means that you have a huge yet often untapped energy source, regardless of whether you are skinny or not.

Do you see how unsustainable a glucose-dependent life is compared to burning fat for fuel? By utilizing fat as a source of energy, you will avoid wild energy and mood swings that usually result from a carb-based diet. You will be able to achieve stable blood sugar and energy levels.

Ways of Maintaining Ketosis

Every individual has their own reasons for choosing to use a Ketogenic diet. However, the most important thing is to make sure that you maintain ketosis during that period. You must learn how to track and monitor your macros. The extra effort always pays off in the end.

There are three major ways of sustaining ketosis:

- **Short-term ketosis** – This is where you only follow a Ketogenic diet for a brief period when you need to achieve a specific result. For some people, staying in ketosis for a long period of time is simply not feasible. Such people can use short-term ketosis to burn fat for a short period of time to reap the benefits without interfering with their lifestyle. This applies to athletic people who may decide to use the Targeted Ketogenic Diet before a workout. Short-term ketosis can also be achieved by using exogenous ketones (supplements).

• **Long-term ketosis** – This is where you maintain ketosis for an extended period of time. Once you have gone through the phases of ketosis, your body becomes keto-adapted and more efficient in utilising ketones for energy. Sustaining long-term ketosis is suited for people who want to maintain good health, heal from long-standing ailments, or lose weight.

• **Cyclical ketosis** – This is a very flexible plan where you eat Ketogenic meals for a couple of days and then switch to consuming more carbs for the next several days. The goal of cyclical ketosis is not to sustain ketosis full time but to maintain flexibility while enjoying some of the benefits of ketosis. This is commonly used by bodybuilders and weightlifters.

How to Sustain Your Ketosis

Here are some tips on how to ensure that your Ketogenic diet is sustainable in the long term:

1. Eat protein in moderation – The Ketogenic diet is essentially a high-fat, moderate protein, and low-carb diet. Most beginners often try to replace their carbs with protein instead of fat. A high-protein diet will not sustain ketosis because the body will prioritize breaking down protein for energy instead of using ketones. To sustain ketosis, keep your protein intake minimal.

2. Learn how to track your carbs – The number of carbs that puts one person in ketosis may not be the same for somebody else. That's why you need to find out exactly how many grams of carbs are right for you.

The easiest way to track your macros is to determine your total daily calorie intake. There are many online resources that can help you do this, such as MyFitnessPal.com or freedieting.com.

3. Know how to test your ketone levels – If tracking your carb intake seems a bit too cumbersome, then you can focus on measuring your ketone levels instead. This will help you check whether you are producing ketones and how much. You can use the blood test, urine test, or breath test described in chapter 2.

Sustaining ketosis requires a great deal of planning, so always stay on your toes when it comes to regular ketone tests and tracking carbs. Things may be a bit messy in the beginning due to trial and error, but once you have established some sort of baseline, things will get much easier for you.

The important thing to achieving sustainable ketosis is to avoid guessing or assuming. Perform routine checks to determine your progress. If you realize that things aren't going your way, review your eating and lifestyle habits. Don't be afraid to try new things like supplements or MCT oil powder. If you need to slash your carb and protein intake further, then try that as well. Your diet is personal, so do whatever seems to work for you.

Foods to Avoid

Part of living a sustainable Ketogenic lifestyle involves knowing which foods to avoid. There are a lot of foods out there that some people claim to be suited for ketosis but aren't really helpful. Fortunately, ketones can be measured, which means that once you eat something, you can determine whether it has put you in ketosis or not. Luckily for you, this chapter contains a comprehensive list of foods that you need to avoid in order to achieve ketosis. This way, you don't have to keep checking your breath or urine after every meal!

Grains

All kinds of grains – including whole grains – must be avoided since they contain a high level of carbs that will prevent ketosis. Examples of such foods include:

- Wheat

- Quinoa

- Buckwheat

- Rice

- Barley

- Sorghum

- Oats

- Corn

- Amaranth

- Rye

- Millet

- Bread, pasta, cookies, pizza crusts, or crackers made from the above

Beans and Legumes

Most beans and legumes contain high starch content, so avoid the following:

- Kidney beans

- Black bean

- Pinto beans

- Lentils

- Lima beans

- Fava beans

- Chickpeas

- White beans

Fruits

Most fruits simply contain too much sugar for the Ketogenic diet and should be avoided. There are a few that you are allowed to consume in small quantities, and examples of these have been listed in the next chapter. Fruits to stay away from include:

- Mangos

- Bananas

- Papaya

- Pineapples

- Oranges

- Tangerines

- Grapes

- Fruit juices, concentrates, syrups, and smoothies

Starchy Vegetables

It is recommended that you avoid any veggies that grow underground and eat leafy greens. This is due to the high levels of starch in some root veggies, which include the following:

- Parsnips

- Potatoes

- Yams

- Yucca

- Sweet potatoes

- Carrots

- Artichoke

Alcohol

This may be a tough one for most people, but alcohol contains contain a lot of carbs which can easily be broken down into sugars in the body. Avoid all alcoholic drinks including beers, cocktails, wines, flavoured liquors, and mixers.

An assortment of alcoholic beverages unsuitable for a Ketogenic diet

Sugars

This may seem obvious, but don't forget that you should also avoid natural sugars and not just the added ones that are found in packed products. Natural sugars to avoid include:

- Cane sugar

- Honey

- Maple syrup

- High fructose corn syrup

- Agave nectar

- Turbinado sugar

Sugar-Alcohols

- Maltitol
- Xylitol
- Sorbitol (found in chewing gum)

Low-Fat Dairy and Milk

Any kind of low-fat dairy product should be avoided because they are low in fat but very high in carbs. Therefore, avoid the following dairy products:

- Milk
- Low-fat and fat-free yoghurts
- Evaporated skim milk
- Low-fat cream cheese
- Fat-free butter
- Shredded cheese

Factory-Farmed Products

- Grain-fed meats
- Factory-farmed fish (These are high in mercury and inflammatory Omega-6 fatty acids)
- Factory-farmed pork
- Hot dogs and packed sausages (These contain nitrates that are potentially cancerous)

Processed Vegetable Oils

- Sunflower oil
- Canola oil
- Sesame oil
- Soybean oil
- Peanut oil
- Grapeseed oil
- Corn oil

Packaged/Processed Foods

These foodstuffs are full of processed oils, preservatives, sugars, and trans fats. They include:

- Margarine
- MSG (Mono Sodium Glutamate)
- Ice creams
- Wheat gluten
- Fast food
- Candies
- Baked goods like cakes and cookies
- Sodas/soft drinks
- Almond milk products
- Dried fruits
- Gelatin

Artificial Sweeteners

These may not be exactly sugar but they sometimes cause blood sugar levels to rise and may give you cravings. This may disrupt your ketosis. Therefore, avoid sweeteners such as:

- Saccharin
- Splenda
- Equal
- Aspartame
- Sucralose
- Acesulfame

Chapter Summary

Here are the key points of the chapter that you need to remember:

- Fats are a more sustainable source of energy than carbs. The human body has more calories of fats than glycogen, and as a fuel, fat provides a more stable blood glucose level than carbs.

- Short-term ketosis can be achieved via a Targeted Ketogenic Diet or by taking exogenous supplements. These are great options for athletes who want to boost performance for an event.

- Long-term ketosis is achieved by sticking to a Ketogenic diet for a long time. Though not feasible for everyone, it works well for those who want to maintain a healthy lifestyle or cure certain long-standing diseases.

- Cyclic ketosis involves following a Ketogenic diet for a few days and then going back to a high-carb diet for several days. This kind of flexibility is preferred by bodybuilders.

- To sustain ketosis, eat protein in moderation, keep track of your carbs, and measure your ketone levels regularly.

- To effectively sustain ketosis, you must know the types of foods to avoid. Some common foods are not suited for a Ketogenic diet and may prevent you from achieving your goals.

In the next chapter, you will learn the appropriate foods that you should eat and some of the delicious recipes that will help you get started on your Ketogenic journey.

Chapter Six: Common Ketogenic Foods and Recipes

In this chapter, you will learn about the foods that you get to enjoy while on the Ketogenic diet. It may seem like the list in the previous chapter practically eliminated all the good stuff, but there are many food options still available to you. You will also learn how to prepare some simple Ketogenic meals using the recipes provided here. There is also information that will help you understand how to calculate nutritional values and distribute your macros throughout the day.

The Ketogenic Food List

The Ketogenic diet isn't as restrictive when you look at the list of foods that you *are* allowed to eat. There's actually a lot of variety here, and if you consider the fact that fats are very filling, you are not likely to go hungry when in ketosis. So long as your body is producing and utilising ketones, you can eat practically anything.

Healthy Animal Fats

- Ghee
- Lard
- Grass-fed butter
- Cream cheese
- Egg yolks
- Tallow
- Organ meat e.g. bone marrow, liver, tongue
- Shellfish e.g. lobster, crab, scallops, squid, shrimp, prawns
- Wild-caught fish e.g. salmon, mackerel, snapper, halibut, tuna, cod, trout, eel

Cooking Oils

- Unrefined coconut oil
- Avocado oil
- Olive oil

Nuts and Seeds

- Walnuts
- Pine nuts
- Pistachios
- Pecans
- Cashews
- Hazelnuts
- Sunflower seeds
- Hemp seeds
- Chia seeds
- Sesame seeds
- Flax oil
- Macadamia oil
- Walnut oil

Vegetables

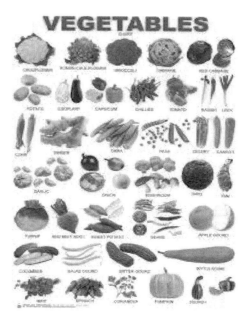

- Celery
- Tomatoes
- Kale
- Brussels sprouts
- Bok Choy
- Onion
- Garlic
- Peppers
- Eggplant
- Cucumber
- Fresh herbs (e.g. cilantro, chives, mint, rosemary, parsley, basil)
- Mushrooms
- Lettuce
- Zucchini
- Endive
- Fennel
- Radicchio

Animal Protein

- Pork
- Chicken
- Beef
- Wild game
- Turkey
- Duck
- Bone Broth

Fruit

- Strawberries
- Blackberries
- Blueberries
- Raspberries
- Apple
- Lime
- Lemon
- Pears

Others/Supplements

- Spirulina
- Mustard
- Mayonnaise
- Sauerkraut
- Allspice
- Pesto
- Dark organic chocolate
- MCT oil
- Almond flour
- Chlorella
- Fish oil supplements
- Maca Root
- Raw cacao powder
- Coconut flour
- Herbal coffee and tea (with no sugar)
- Mineral water or Seltzer
- Unsweetened nut milk e.g. coconut milk, hazelnut milk, cashew milk, hemp milk, almond milk)
- Omega-3
- Magnesium
- Sodium

- Glutamine
- Taurine
- BCAAs (Branch Chain Amino Acids)
- Whey protein
- Essential amino acids

Carb Timing

Though there is no specific recommendation of meal timings with a Ketogenic diet, there are some factors that you may need to consider when trying to distribute your macros throughout the day.

When it comes to carb consumption, you should try to eat them at the end of the day rather than in the mornings. When you eat carbs in the morning, your blood sugar goes up, and this may lead to fluctuations during the rest of the day. Therefore, enjoy a high-fat and moderate-protein meal for breakfast and lunch and then save your carbs for dinner.

Ketogenic Meal Plans and Recipes

The meal plans and recipes below are designed for people who are just starting out on a Ketogenic diet. They are simple and easy to make so that you don't have to worry too much about whether you're going to get it right. They have been categorised into the three main meals of the day and some snacks have also been thrown in.

The Ketogenic diet doesn't really have fixed eating times. You can eat whenever you feel like it, provided that you restrict your carbs to less than 50 grams a day and set definite targets for your protein levels.

If you normally have three meals a day, then you may have to distribute your carb and protein intake across the three meals. To calculate the nutritional values of your meals, you can use an online calculator.

Here is a seven-day meal plan that can help you get started for your first week.

Meal Plan for Day 1

Breakfast – Ketogenic Green Smoothie

Lunch – Tamari Marinated Steak Salad

Dinner – Garlic Ghee Pan-Fried Cod

Meal Plan for Day 2

Breakfast – Low-Carb Pancake Donuts

Lunch – Garlic Chicken Wrapped in Bacon

Dinner – Avocado Tuna Salad

Meal Plan for Day 3

Breakfast – Lemon Thyme Muffins

Lunch – Mustard Sardines Salad

Dinner – Beef Curry

Meal Plan for Day 4

Breakfast – Pesto Scrambled Eggs

Lunch – Spicy Thai Meatballs

Dinner – Thai Chicken and Rice

Meal Plan for Day 5

Breakfast – Ham and Mushroom Scramble

Lunch –Zucchini Avocado Burger

Dinner – Pork Tenderloin

Meal Plan for Day 6

Breakfast – Coconut and Ghee Coffee

Lunch – Bacon and Broccoli Salad

Dinner – Stir-Fried Almond Spinach

Meal Plan for Day 7

Breakfast - Chicken Soup with Poached Egg

Lunch - Zucchini Beef Saute

Dinner – Grilled Chicken Skewers

Breakfast Recipes

Ketogenic Green Smoothie

How about a green smoothie to start your day? This drink will leave you refreshed and energized in no time!

Yield: 1

Ingredients:
2 Brazil nuts
10 almonds
2 cups kale or spinach
1 cup unsweetened coconut milk
1 scoop Amazing Grass Greens Powder

Method:
1. Blend the almonds, Brazil nuts, and coconut milk until it forms a puree.
2. Toss in the remaining ingredients and blend well.

Nutritional Values:
Calories – 380

Fat – 30 grams
Protein – 12 grams
Net Carbs – 16 grams
Fibre – 8 grams

Low-Carb Pancake Donuts

Here are some low-carb pancakes to get you fired up in the morning.

Yield: 4

Ingredients:
4 Tbsp almond flour
1 tsp coconut flour
1 tsp baking powder
1 tsp vanilla extract
3 large eggs
85 grams (3 oz) cream cheese
Coconut oil for cooking

Method:

    1. Pour the ingredients into a large bowl. Use an immersion blender to mix all the ingredients together.

    2. Take a doughnut-maker and spray the surface with the coconut oil. Heat up the doughnut-maker and pour some batter into each well.

    3. Cook for 3 minutes on one side and then flip the doughnut over. Cook for 2 more minutes.

4. Remove the doughnut and repeat the process using the remaining batter.

5. Serve

Nutritional Values Per Serving:
Calories – 32
Fats – 2.7 grams
Protein – 1.4 grams
Carbs – 0.4 grams
Fibre – 0 grams

Lemon Thyme Muffins

Here is a delicious recipe that will make you enough tasty muffins for the entire family.

Yield: 12

Ingredients:
4 eggs
3 cups almond flour
½ cup melted ghee
1 cup bacon bits
1 tsp baking soda
2 tsp lemon thyme
½ tsp salt

Method:

1. Preheat the oven to 180° C (350° F).

2. Pour the melted ghee, almond flour, and baking soda into a mixing bowl.

3. Add the eggs, lemon thyme, and salt.

4. Mix the ingredients well.

5. Toss in the bits of bacon.

6. Line a muffin pan using muffin liners. Scoop the batter into the pan until it is ¾ full.

7. Bake for 20 minutes.

8. Serve warm

Nutritional Values Per Serving:

Calories – 300

Fat – 28 grams

Protein – 11 grams

Carbs – 8 grams

Fibre – 3 grams

Pesto Scrambled Eggs

Get ready to enjoy some yummy eggs with cream and butter.

Yield: 1

Ingredients:
3 large eggs
2 Tbsp soured cream
1 Tbsp pesto
1 Tbsp grass-fed butter
Salt and black pepper to taste

Method:

1. Crack the eggs into a bowl and add the salt and black pepper. Whisk the mixture well.

2. Pour the mixture into a pan and then toss in the butter. Heat the pan over low heat.

3. Stir constantly to keep the eggs creamy. Add the pesto and keep stirring.

4. Remove the pan from the heat and pour the soured cream into the egg mixture. Mix well.

5. Serve with avocado slices.

Nutritional Values:
Calories – 467
Fat – 41.5 grams
Protein – 20.4 grams
Carbs – 2.6 grams
Fibre – 0.7 grams

Ham and Mushroom Scramble

A delightful ham and mushroom dish that will warm your palate any day!

Yield: 1

Ingredients:
4 baby Bella mushrooms
2 slices ham
3 eggs
½ cup spinach
¼ cup red bell peppers
1 Tbsp coconut oil
Salt and pepper

Method:

1. Chop the ham and vegetables.
2. Pour ½ tablespoon of coconut oil into a pan and sauté the ham and vegetables
3. Crack the eggs into a bowl and whisk well. Pour the remaining ½ tablespoon of coconut oil into another pan and cook the scramble the eggs over medium heat.
4. Stir the eggs constantly until they cook, and then add salt and pepper to taste.
5. Finally, pour the sautéed ham and vegetables over the eggs and mix.
6. Serve hot.

Nutritional Values:
Calories – 350
Fat – 29 grams
Protein – 21 grams
Carbohydrates – 9 grams
Fibre – 1 gram

Lunch Recipes

Tamari Marinated Steak Salad

This saucy steak will leave you begging for more. Hey, if it fits your macros, why not?

Yield: 2

Ingredients:
250 grams (1/2 lb) steak
2 handfuls (75 grams or 2.5 oz) salad greens
4 radishes, sliced
6 grape tomatoes, halved
½ red bell pepper, sliced

½ Tbsp fresh lemon juice
½ Tbsp olive oil
¼ cup gluten-free Tamari soy sauce
Avocado oil
Salt to taste

Method:

1. Use the Tamari soy sauce to marinade the steak.
2. Place the pepper slices, radishes, tomatoes, and greens in a bowl and toss with the lemon juice, olive oil, and salt.
3. Serve the salad on two plates.
4. Place a frying pan on high heat, pour some avocado oil, and cook the steak to your liking.
5. Allow the steak to cool for 1 minute. Slice the steak and share out between the two salad plates.
6. Serve.

Nutritional Values per Serving:
Calories – 500
Fat – 37 grams
Protein – 33 grams
Carbs – 5 grams
Fibre – 2 grams

Garlic Chicken Wrapped in Bacon

Chicken wrapped in bacon? Can a dish get more Keto than this?

Yield: 4

Ingredients:

3 Tbsp garlic powder
8 slices bacon, sliced into thirds
1 chicken breast chopped into bite-sized pieces

Method:

1. Preheat the oven to 205° Celsius (400° F).
2. Use aluminium foil to line a baking tray.
3. Pour the garlic powder into a small bowl and dip every chicken piece into the powder.
4. Wrap each piece of chicken with a bacon slice. Place the wrapped chicken pieces on the tray without touching each other.
5. Bake for 15 minutes and then turn the pieces over. The bacon should turn crispy.
6. Skewer each piece with a toothpick and serve.

Nutritional Values per Serving:

Calories – 230

Fat – 13 grams

Protein – 22 grams

Carbs – 7 grams

Fibre – 1 gram

Mustard Sardines Salad

This is a simple fish meal that is quick and easy to make.

Yield: 1

Ingredients:
¼ cucumber, peeled and diced
½ Tbsp mustard
1 Tbsp lemon juice
1 can sardines
Salt and pepper to taste

Method:
1. Pour the sardines into a bowl and mash them up. Make sure you drain out most of the olive oil from the can.
2. Add the cucumbers, mustard, melon juice, salt, and pepper.
3. Mix all the ingredients together.
4. Serve.

Nutritional Value:
Calories – 260 grams
Fat – 20 grams
Protein – 25 grams
Carbs – 0 grams

Bacon and Broccoli Salad

If you love bacon, then you will adore this creamy dish. A filling meal that is fit for a family dinner.

Yield: 6

Ingredients:
20 bacon slices, chopped
500 grams (1 lb) broccoli florets
1 cup coconut cream
2 red onions, sliced
Salt to taste

Method:
1. Fry the chopped bacon in a pan and then use the bacon fat to cook the onions.
2. Boil the broccoli until soft.
3. Mix the bacon, onions, and broccoli together.
4. Add the coconut cream and salt.
5. Serve.

Nutritional Value per Serving:
Calories – 280
Fat – 26 grams
Protein – 7 grams
Carbohydrates – 10 grams
Fibre – 3 grams

Zucchini Avocado Burgers

Instead of using regular buns, this creative Keto dish uses zucchini slices to make the burgers.

Yield: 2

Ingredients:
225 grams (½ lb) ground beef
1 large zucchini
¼ avocado
1 Tbsp mustard
1 Tbsp mayonnaise
2 Tbsp avocado oil
2 tsp salt

Method:
1. Preheat the oven to 200° C (400° F).
2. Spray a baking tray with avocado oil and sprinkle salt over it.
3. Chop the zucchini into ½-inch slices and place them on the tray.

91

4. Create eight small meatballs from the beef and then form patties. Place the patties on the tray.

5. Place the baking tray into the oven for 15 minutes.

6. As the patties bake, cut the avocado into thin slices.

7. Put together the burgers using the zucchini slices as buns. Top each beef patty with a slice of avocado, mayonnaise, and mustard.

8. Serve warm.

Nutritional Value per Serving:

Calories – 370

Fat – 30 grams

Protein – 23 grams

Carbs – 13 grams

Fibre – 6 grams

Dinner Recipes

Garlic Ghee Pan-Fried Cod

The ghee and garlic add a unique and wonderful flavour to the fish fillet. It's simply delicious.

Yield: 4

Ingredients:
6 garlic cloves, minced
3 Tbsp ghee

4 cod fillets (0.3 lb each)
Salt to taste

Method:
1. Place a frying pan over medium heat and melt the ghee.
2. Pour half the garlic into the pan.
3. Cook the fillets on one side and sprinkle the salt over the fish.
4. When the cod fillets turn solid white halfway up the side, flip them over and pour in the remaining minced garlic.
5. Cook until the entire fillet turns white and flaky.
6. Serve together with the ghee and garlic from the pan.

Nutritional Values per Serving:
Calories – 160
Fat – 7 grams
Protein – 21 grams
Carbs – 1 gram
Fibre – 0 grams

Avocado Tuna Salad

The avocado, cucumber, and salad greens give what would be a potentially plain dish a splash of colour.

Yield: 1

Ingredients:
½ small avocado, finely diced
1 can (150 grams or 6 oz) of tuna
1/3 cucumber, finely diced
Salad greens
1 tsp lemon juice
1 Tbsp mustard
1 Tbsp Paleo mayo
Black pepper and salt to taste

Method:
1. Mix the diced avocado and cucumber in a bowl and add the lemon juice.
2. In a separate bowl, flake the tuna and then pour in the mustard and mayo. Mix well.

3. Pour the tuna into the bowl of avocado and cucumber.

4. Prepare your salad greens.

5. Pour the tuna salad over the salad greens.

6. Flavour with salt and black pepper.

7. Serve.

Nutritional Values per Serving:

Calories – 480

Fat – 40 grams

Protein – 45 grams

Carbs – 13 grams

Fibre – 8 grams

Beef Curry

This extra spicy traditional beef dish is guaranteed to get your metabolism all fired up.

Yield: 4

Ingredients:
500 grams (1 lb) boneless short-ribs
¾ cup coconut milk
¼ cup basil leaves, chopped
2 cloves garlic, minced
1 medium onion, sliced
1 tsp grated ginger
1 tsp ground coriander
1 Tbsp fish sauce
1 Tbsp curry powder
1 tsp cardamom
1 tsp ground turmeric
1 tsp ground cumin
Salt to taste
Coconut oil for cooking

Method:

1. Place a saucepan over medium heat and pour in some coconut oil. Sauté the onions and short-ribs for 5 minutes until the beef turns brown.

2. Pour the coconut milk, fish sauce, and spices into the saucepan. Boil the mixture, cover with a lid and simmer for 1 hour.

3. Toss in the ginger, garlic, basil, and salt. Simmer for an additional 10 minutes.

4. Serve.

Nutritional Values per Serving:
Calories – 440
Fat – 33 grams
Protein – 25 grams
Carbs – 13 grams
Fibre – 4 grams

Thai Chicken and Rice

If you are looking to replace rice in your menu, cauliflower makes a great substitute. See how this spicy meal is put together with minimal fuss.

Yield: 4

Ingredients:
3 eggs
4 cooked chicken breasts, shredded
1 head cauliflower
½ cup cilantro, chopped
1 Tbsp grated ginger
1 Tbsp coconut aminos
3 cloves garlic, crushed
3 chillies
Salt to taste
Coconut oil for cooking

Method:

    1.   Divide the cauliflower into florets and place in a food processor. Blend until you get a rice-like texture. You may have to process the florets in batches.

2. Place a large pan over medium heat and pour the coconut oil into the pan. Cook the cauliflower rice in batches. Stir regularly.

3. Take another pan and scramble the eggs in coconut oil. Pour the eggs over the cooked cauliflower rice.

4. Add chopped chillies, garlic, and ginger.

5. Once the cauliflower softens, add the shredded chicken.

6. Add the coconut aminos and salt. Mix well.

7. Garnish with chopped cilantro.

8. Serve.

Nutritional Values per Serving:

Calories – 350

Fat – 11 grams

Protein – 55 grams

Carbs – 13 grams

Fibre – 4 grams

Pork Tenderloin

Pig out on this sumptuous dinner loaded with healthy fats and no carbs whatsoever.

Yield: 2

Ingredients:
500 grams (1 lb) pork tenderloin
1 Tbsp coconut oil
Salt and pepper

Method:

1. Slice the tenderloin into two equal halves.
2. Place a pan over medium heat and melt the coconut oil.
3. Cook the pork pieces in the pan. Keep turning the pork until each side is well cooked.

4. Use a meat thermometer to check the internal temperature of the pork. It should be just below 63° C (145° F).

5. Set the pork aside to cool as it will still be cooking even after you remove it from the pan.

6. After a few minutes, slice the pork into 1-inch slices and serve.

Nutritional Values per Serving:
Calories – 330
Fat – 15 grams
Protein – 47 grams
Carbs – 0 grams
Fibre – 0 grams

Chapter Summary

Here are the key points of the chapter:

- Most people think the Ketogenic diet is too restrictive. However, there are a lot of healthy foods that can help you produce and utilise ketones.

- There are no specific rules for meal timings, but you should try to eat most of your carbs toward the end of the day. This will help you avoid blood sugar fluctuations.

- Online nutritional calculators are very useful for calculating your macros and nutritional values of your meals.

In the next chapter, you will learn how ketosis affects your workouts and how you can enhance your physical performance while on a Ketogenic diet.

Chapter Seven: Exercise and Ketosis

In this chapter, you will learn how to exercise while on a Ketogenic diet. Many people wonder how it's possible to achieve maximum physical performance without carbs, so you will learn some of the ways of depending on ketones when exercising. Let's start by busting some common myths about carbs and exercise.

Common Myths

The first myth we need to clear up is that avoiding carbs will negatively impact your physical performance. This is partially true, but only during the initial phases of keto-adaptation. During this transitional period, your performance will drop to some extent, though this will only last a few weeks. After that initial 3-week adaptation period, your body will have switched from burning glucose to utilizing ketones and fatty acids for energy.

Many studies have been conducted on the impact a Ketogenic diet has on strength and endurance athletes. In one study, eight athletes were put on a zero-carb diet for a period of 30 days. The results showed that this did not affect their strength performance negatively at all. Many other studies are now showing just how beneficial keto-adaptation is for athletes.

Another myth is that a Ketogenic diet will prevent you from gaining muscle or even result in muscle loss. This myth is driven by the belief that, in order to gain muscle, you must eat carbs to trigger insulin production. The truth is that a Ketogenic diet will actually spare your muscles from being broken down for energy.

The truth is that gaining muscle on a Ketogenic diet may be slower than when eating carbs. However, the upside is that you won't gain as much fat, so it's definitely worth it. Of course, if you happen to be a powerlifter or bodybuilder, then you will obviously need to load up on carbs prior to some of your workouts. For the average person, this may not be necessary. Everyone's body is different, so while some can work out on the Standard Ketogenic Diet, others may perform better with the Targeted or Cyclic Ketogenic Diets.

Carb Loading

Carb loading is simply a technique where you eat a lot of carbs right before you start your workout to boost your performance. This is not something that is recommended for everyone on a Ketogenic diet. Whether to carb load or not will depend on your personal goals, such as weight loss, muscle gain, or strength and endurance.

Carb Loading and Fat Loss

Do you need to eat more carbs when aiming for fat loss? If your goal is to lose fat or maintain your weight, you do not need to stock up on carbs at all. You should follow the Standard Ketogenic Diet, where you consume only 20 to 50 grams of net carbs daily. You have enough fat reserves in your body to help you produce energy, but in case you need an energy boost minus the carbs, you can take some coconut oil or MCT oil.

Personalised nutrition is very important when you are following a Ketogenic diet. This means that you have to find what will work for you instead of relying on general recommendations. For example, some people are able to tolerate MCT oil while others tend to experience some kind of stomach discomfort.

The bottom line is that if you are keen on losing fat or maintaining your weight, you do not need to carb load. You should only consider eating more carbs when you want to engage in very intense exercises for a long period of time.

Carb Loading and Muscle Gain

Do you need to carb load when trying to gain more muscle? Well, that depends on your fitness goals. There are different variations of the Ketogenic diet that actually allow for increased carb consumption.

If you follow the Targeted Ketogenic Diet (TKD), which is primarily used by advanced athletes who are engaging in high-intensity activities, carb loading should be strategically scheduled around your workouts. This will allow you to boost performance without interfering with ketosis in the long term. Just make sure that you avoid loading up on carbs that are high in fructose. Choose foods that contain glucose or dextrose because these sugars will be used up quickly by the body to provide muscle glycogen. The problem with fructose is that it is stored in form of liver glycogen, which will end up interrupting ketosis.

If you follow the Cyclic Ketogenic Diet (CKD), which is preferred by professional athletes like bodybuilders, you can eat low-carb meals for a number of days and then switch to high-carb foods for several days.

If you aren't into lifting heavy weights, then leave CKD to the pros

It should be clear by now that both these Ketogenic variations are meant only for specific types of people. The TKD and CKD variations can only work for people who are already lean. The CKD approach can also be very tricky for the average person because you may easily consume too many carbs.

Carb Loading and High Intensity Interval Training (HIIT)

HIIT is an explosive form of exercise where you engage in intense power, fitness, and strength exercises with very little rest periods in between. You are essentially exerting a near-maximum force on your body through intense body movements.

So, do you need to eat a lot of carbs for HIIT exercises? That will depend on the kind of exercises you plan on engaging in. Most people do not need extra carbs either before or after their workouts. However, if you are performing Crossfit, sprints, or other explosive exercises, you may need to consume extra carbs to sustain your strength.

Types of Exercise

As we have already seen, your nutritional needs are personal and dependent on the type of exercise you perform. There are four types of exercises that you can do in ketosis:

1. Aerobic exercises – These are also known as cardio exercises, and usually last more than three minutes. You can engage in low-intensity cardio workouts to help you burn fat. Ensure that you stretch your workout sessions instead of trying to squeeze everything into a short window of time.

A long jog is a good aerobic activity

107

2.Anaerobic exercises – These are workouts that are performed in short bursts and require a lot of energy, for example, HIIT and lifting weights. You will need to eat more carbs before performing anaerobic exercises since fat alone cannot provide adequate energy for these exercises.

High Intensity Interval Training exercise

3. Flexibility exercises – These exercises help in stretching your muscles, enhancing your muscular range of motion, and providing support for your joints. Flexibility exercises include yoga and post-workout stretches. They are very helpful in enhancing your flexibility and preventing injuries that result from the shortening of muscles.

Stretch before and after your workout

4.Stability exercises – These include core training and balance exercises, such as planks, bridges, and stability balls. They boost the strength of muscles, improve body alignment, and help control body movement.

Balancing exercise

The bottom line here is that as long as you are in ketosis, you need to consider the intensity of your workouts. Remember that low-intensity aerobic exercises will burn fat as the primary source of energy, while high-intensity aerobic exercises usually require carbs as the primary energy source. Since ketosis naturally burns fat to produce energy, you may find it difficult to engage in high-intensity (anaerobic) workouts at the beginning of the Ketogenic diet. However, you can decide to use the Targeted Ketogenic Diet to help you cope.

How to Use the TKD Approach

The Standard Ketogenic Diet may not help you much if you are constantly engaging in intense workouts. If you happen to be exercising for more than three days every week either through sprints or weightlifting, you must find another way to meet your carb needs without compromising ketosis.

You can adopt the Targeted Ketogenic Diet but only for your intense workout days. You can eat between 15 and 30 grams of carbs from sources like bananas, raisins, and blueberries. These are known as *fast-acting carbs* because the glucose they provide is absorbed very quickly into the tissues and therefore will not interfere with ketosis. Make sure that you eat these carbs 30 minutes to one hour prior to your workout and then after your workout as well. This will help you gain enough muscle glycogen to push through your workout while also boosting recovery post-exercise.

On the days when you are not working out or are simply engaging in light aerobic, flexibility, or stability exercises, you can go back to following the Standard Ketogenic Diet.

Benefits of Exercising in Ketosis

Now that we have cleared up the issue of whether ketosis is an obstacle to exercise, let's look at some of the significant benefits of exercising while in ketosis:

- A research study was conducted on two groups of ultra-endurance athletes. One group had been eating a low-carb diet for about two years while the other group had been living on a high-carb diet. They were then asked to go on a three-hour run. The results showed that the athletes who had been following a low-carb diet were able to burn 2-3 times more fat than the other group. This proves that combining a Ketogenic diet with exercise will help you burn fat at a faster rate compared to someone who exercises on a high-carb diet.

- It would be easy to assume that the high-carb group would have more muscle glycogen at their disposal since they are used to eating more carbs. However, the same study showed that the low-carb athletes still used the same quantity of muscle glycogen as the others. In other words, they had access to just as much energy as the high-carb group.

- Ketosis helps to prevent fatigue when performing long aerobic exercises.

- Research shows that when obese individuals <u>combine ketosis with exercise</u>, they can maintain their blood glucose levels better.

Though exercising in ketosis has been viewed negatively for years due to the mainstream belief that carbs are necessary to boost performance, the truth is that a Ketogenic diet can fit into an active lifestyle. Whether you work out at a low, moderate, or high intensity, all you have to do is tweak the Standard Ketogenic Diet a little bit to find a way to personalise it. Just make sure you don't go overboard with your carbs and interfere with ketosis.

Chapter Summary

Here are the key points of the chapter that you need to remember:

- You do not need to eat a lot of carbs to work out.

- The Ketogenic diet does not have a negative impact on your physical performance when exercising. Studies show that you can preserve or even gain muscle while on a Ketogenic diet.

- Carb loading involves consuming more than the standard amount of carbs for a Ketogenic diet in order to boost your workout performance. It is done either days or hours before an intense workout.

- Ensure that you personalise your nutrition instead of copying others. People respond differently to exercise while in ketosis, so find something that fits your needs.

- If you are thinking of loading up on carbs, consider the type of exercise you are going to engage in.

- There are four styles of exercises that you can perform with a Ketogenic diet: aerobic, anaerobic, flexibility, and stability exercises. You may need to eat more carbs when performing anaerobic exercises because of the intense workouts involved.

- The TKD is best suited for workout days. Make sure you consume 15 to 30 grams of fast-acting carbohydrates at least 30 minutes before and after your workout. Go for bananas, berries, and raisins.

- Some of the benefits of combining ketosis with exercise include faster fat loss, prevention of fatigue during extended

112

aerobic exercises, and better blood glucose balance in obese individuals.

In the next chapter, you will learn about some of the misconceptions regarding the Ketogenic diet and the mistakes you need to avoid to get the results you want.

Chapter Eight: Common Myths and Mistakes

In this chapter, you will learn about some of the common myths that many people have regarding the Ketogenic diet. You will also learn some of the mistakes that you need to avoid if you want to achieve your goals with the Ketogenic diet.

The Great Myths

There are two great myths that we will tackle in this chapter. The first has to do with fats and the second is a condition known as ketoacidosis.

Myth #1: Eating Fat Makes You Fat

Have you ever heard of the phrase, "You are what you eat?" This is something that nutritionists say when they want to advise their patients to avoid certain foods that are bad for their health. However, many people have used this statement out of context by implying that if you eat fat then you will become fat. This is simply not true.

The truth is that fat is not the enemy when it comes to excessive weight gain. If fat was indeed the problem, then someone would be able to eat cereal and drink 10 sodas with every meal and still stay lean. How many people do you know who eat like that and are still lean? Unless you are somehow extremely sensitive to insulin, this is highly improbable.

All our lives, we have been conditioned to believe that a diet consisting of high amounts of fat leads to life-threatening diseases such as diabetes, obesity, heart disease, and high blood pressure. Consequently, very few people are willing to embrace a lifestyle that advocates for the consumption of a lot of butter and bacon. Well, if fat was the major cause of obesity and all these other lifestyle diseases, then the statistics would prove it. However, a simple glance at the rates of obesity in the US paints a very peculiar picture.

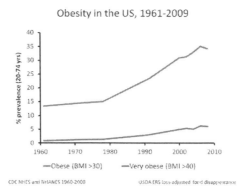

Looking at the graph above, you will notice that the obesity levels were pretty much stable from the 1960s all the way to 1980. After that, there seems to be a sudden spike and the percentage of people who are classified as obese or very obese almost doubles in just 10 years. So, what happened in the 1980s?

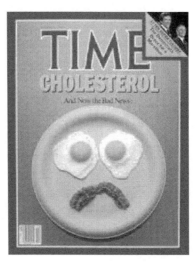

The low-fat craze that gripped the world in the 1980s

115

During the 80s, there was a push by health professionals and food marketers to convince people to stop eating fatty foods. They came up with nutritional guidelines that led the public to believe that consuming fat would lead to serious weight gain and many other health complications. All of a sudden, almost every food item had a low-fat option. It was as if fat was a plague and needed to be avoided at all costs.

As you can see from the graph, the public's health conditions didn't improve as they should have. People were eating more "low-fat" food options, especially those that were already packaged as such, but obesity rates were climbing really fast. Society was getting fatter every year despite the low-fat recommendations. So, what was the cause of this phenomenon?

Years later, some scientists decided to pinpoint why more people were suffering from obesity and other metabolic problems. Was it the carbohydrates, the fat, or something else?

A study was conducted where the test subject's blood was infused with fat alone. In the next stage of the study, the test subject's blood was infused with both fat and carbohydrates. The results showed that when fat alone is infused into the subject's blood, it was utilized by the body as a source of fuel. There was also a distinct lack of any spike in glucose or insulin levels, which are usually early warning signs of obesity.

However, the results of the second stage showed that when fat and carbohydrates are both infused into the blood, the body fails to properly utilize the fat as well as the carbohydrates as energy sources. In other words, the body's ability to utilize both fat and carbs was impaired.

This shows that fat on its own cannot make you fat. The problem is the combination of foods that contain high amounts of both fat and carbohydrates. Isn't this what makes up the majority of fast-food meals?

The reality is that a high-fat and low-carb diet will lead to a reduction in insulin production, loss of body fat, and a general improvement in your health.

Myth #2: Ketoacidosis and Ketosis are the same

Most people who have something against a Ketogenic diet usually say that they fear developing ketoacidosis. The misconception here is that they are confusing ketosis with ketoacidosis. We know what ketosis means, but what is ketoacidosis?

Ketoacidosis is the unregulated production of ketones in the bloodstream. During ketoacidosis, ketone levels in the blood rise to an extremely high level of more than 15 mmol/L. Blood glucose and acidity levels also increase dramatically. However, the biggest threat that ketoacidosis poses is the significant rise in blood acidity.

So, is there reason to fear a Ketogenic diet because of ketoacidosis? The truth is that there is nothing to fear — as long as you are a healthy individual who doesn't suffer from Type 1 diabetes. People who suffer from Type 1 diabetes are unable to produce any insulin. When such a person consumes a meal packed with carbohydrates, there is no insulin produced by the pancreas to transport the blood glucose into the cells to generate energy. The blood glucose concentration shoots up from the normal 80 – 100 mg/dL to a whopping 300 mg/dL!

The cells need glucose to produce energy, but there is none coming in. The blood glucose is simply floating around in the blood with no insulin to move it into the cells.

Therefore, the liver begins to break down fats into fatty acids and ketones. Unfortunately, since there is no insulin to control the concentration of ketones produced, the liver keeps on making more and more.

The kidneys are also unable to filter all the glucose out of the bloodstream and it ultimately gets excreted in the urine. Since the glucose hasn't been filtered properly, it ends up absorbing water out of the bloodstream on its way out in the urine. This causes the diabetic person to suffer from low blood volume with a high ketone concentration. Since ketones are made from fatty acids, they are slightly acidic.

117

So now you have a situation where blood glucose levels are elevated, ketone concentration is too high, and the blood is too acidic. Such a condition is what is referred to as ketoacidosis. It can lead to dehydration, swelling in the brain, and even death if it is not treated in time.

What is important to note is that only those who have Type 1 diabetes can develop ketoacidosis. Such people should avoid the Ketogenic diet because they do not have the insulin to control ketone production. If you are a healthy individual, there is nothing to fear at all.

Ketogenic Mistakes to Avoid

If you have chosen to follow a Ketogenic diet, then you need to know some of the potential pitfalls that you must avoid. There are certain mistakes that can send you the wrong way and ruin your health goals. Some of them have to do with your lifestyle while others are simply dietary errors that stem from misinformation and ignorance.

Here are eight major mistakes that you need to avoid:

Mistake #1: Failing to Give Your Body an Adaptation Period

One of the biggest mistakes you can make is to move from a high-carb diet to a low-carb one without allowing yourself a transition period. Your body needs time to adapt to the new source of energy and the different types of foods you will be consuming. Consuming too much fat too quickly without an adaptation period may sometimes result in unexpected bowel movements, which needless to say, can be quite embarrassing.

Some people who go through this automatically assume that a Ketogenic diet is not for them and decide to quit. However, the problem isn't the diet or your body. You have simply not allowed yourself time for keto-adaptation to take place.

The right thing to do is to slowly increase fat consumption over time. This will ensure a smooth transition from the oxidation of glucose to oxidation of fat. Ketones may be present in the bloodstream but the levels are not as stable yet, so take it easy. There are certain negative side effects that you will experience, such as tiredness and headaches, but these are temporary issues.

It is recommended that you start shopping for foods and snacks that are aligned with a Ketogenic diet. Good options include almond butter, flax crackers, and nuts. These will prevent extreme hunger pangs while helping you achieve ketosis.

Mistake #2: Not Consuming Enough Water, Vitamins, and Minerals

During the initial phase of the Ketogenic diet, you are going to lose a lot of water in the form of urine. This water is excreted together with many mineral salts, especially sodium, magnesium, and potassium. Therefore, you must ensure that you constantly replenish these lost electrolytes to stay healthy.

Take enough water and mineral salts to replenish lost electrolytes

Failure to replenish these lost electrolytes is the reason why some people develop "keto-flu," which is a condition where you feel like you are coming down with the flu. In most cases, we are advised to avoid eating too much salt, but when you are in ketosis, you need to take two teaspoons of table salt every day. This will help you maintain your sodium levels. When it comes to drinking water, makes sure that you pay careful attention to your needs. If you are sweating a lot or live in a hot area, then you need to drink even more water.

To get enough potassium and magnesium, consume foods such as beef and vegetable broth. Powdered drinks and pickle juice are also great options. Another key component of the Ketogenic diet is vitamin D, which can be found in fatty fish like tuna and mackerel, beef liver, cheese, and egg yolks. Don't forget that you can always get some multivitamin supplements to boost your vitamin and mineral intake.

Mistake #3: Restricting Total Carbs Instead of Net Carbs

Since the beginning of this book, the word "carbs" has been used to refer to carbohydrates. However, some people who start following a Ketogenic diet don't really understand that there is a difference between total carbs and net carbs. For this reason, many dieters restrict their consumption of total carbs, which is not something that you want to do. But what is the difference between total and net carbs?

There are three main components in carbohydrates – starch, sugar, and fibre. In a Ketogenic diet, you want to restrict the amount of starch and sugar you consume but not your fibre intake. Starch and sugar make up your digestible carbs while fibre is considered to be an indigestible carb. When we talk about total carbs, we are referring to all three components, but net carbs refer only to the two digestible carbs. In other words, you need to restrict your net and not your total carb consumption. In a Ketogenic diet, you can go ahead and eat as much fibre as you want.

Remember that your net carb intake should be around 20 – 50 grams a day.

Mistake #4: Eating Processed Ketogenic Meals

One major aspect of the Ketogenic diet is that you need to stick to real foods. This means that you should only consume foods that are made from real ingredients and not a store-bought product that is already packed.

The problem with most of these pre-packed meals is that they contain a lot of hidden sugars, bad fats, and starch. They may be convenient for you if you live a busy lifestyle, but they will not help you achieve whatever health or weight loss goals you may have. It is always recommended that your Ketogenic meals be made from natural ingredients and are cooked properly, and the best way to be sure about this is to cook the food yourself.

Now, if cooking isn't really your thing, then you may have to look for health food restaurants where you can get Ketogenic meals prepared for you. Just make sure that you always ask about the ingredients that went into your food. There are grocery stores where you can buy pre-cooked dishes such as steamed shrimps, beef briskets, or roasted chicken. If you add some salad and cream dressing, you can make yourself a Ketogenic meal.

There are times when you may be forced to grab a packaged Ketogenic snack like an Atkins bar, but never make these poor nutritional substitutes a priority. Making your own meals is simply the only way to live a sustainable Ketogenic lifestyle.

Mistake #5: Eating Very Little Dietary Fat

You obviously know by now that a Ketogenic diet is a high-fat diet. So, why would you claim to be following this diet yet you are afraid of eating enough fatty foods?

You will have to get used to consuming foods containing a lot of fat!

We have already cleared up the misconception that fatty foods make us fat, so there's no need to discuss this again. Being overweight is usually an issue of consuming too many sugary and starchy foods. The Ketogenic diet seeks to reverse excessive weight gain by turning your body into a natural fat-burning machine, and this is only possible by significantly increasing your fat intake and cutting your carb consumption.

A diet where you restrict your carb consumption *and* limit your fat intake is NOT a Ketogenic diet. Though there are no strict rules about consumption of dietary fat, ensure that at least 80 percent of your macros are from fat. The great thing about meals that contain a lot of fat is that they will keep you full for a very long time. Fat is usually digested very slowly, so you may find that you aren't as hungry as you used to be.

Mistake #6: Consuming the Wrong Type of Fats

Once you decide that you are all-in with eating as much fat as possible, you need to be able to know the difference between the good kind of fat and the bad kind. There are some types of fats that you must simply stay away from.

Let's start with the bad fats that you need to avoid. First of all, any type of fat or oil that is packed in a plastic container is not suited for a Ketogenic diet. Most vegetable and seed oils fall into this category. Another type of fat that is really dangerous for your health is trans fats. These are actually manufactured in a lab and are then used as food preservatives to make food last longer on store shelves. These types of fats are known to cause ailments such as diabetes, heart disease, stroke, and inflammation. Trans fats are normally used with foods such as French fries, crackers, chips, margarine, pastries, cookies, and many other fried foods.

Nutrition Facts

Serv. Size 4 cookies (32g)
Servings 9
Calories 150
Calories from fat 60

Amount/Serving	%DV*	Amount/Serving	%DV*
Total Fat 7g	11%	Total Carb. 20g	7%
Sat. Fat 4.5g	23%	Dietary Fiber 1g	4%
Trans Fat 0g		Sugars 10g	
Cholest. 0mg	0%	Protein 2g	
Sodium 115mg	5%		

Vitamin A 0% • Vitamin C 0% • Calcium 0% • Iron 4%

INGREDIENTS: Enriched flour, riboflavin, sugar, partially hydrogenated vegetable oil, cocoa, cornstarch, hydrogenated oils, soy lecithin, salt, caramel color, artificial flavors.

Read labels when shopping and stay away from Trans fat and partially hydrogenated oil

How can you know that a particular food item contains these bad fats? You need to learn how to check the labels of everything you buy at the store. If something contains an ingredient such as *partially hydrogenated oil*, do not buy it.

Examples of good fats include monounsaturated fats, saturated fats, and specific seeds and fruits. A more detailed list of foods containing good fats has already been provided in Chapter 5.

Mistake #7: Eating Too Much Protein

Protein forms a very important component of any diet because the body cannot synthesise all the essential amino acids necessary for the development of organs and muscles. However, there's a reason why a Ketogenic diet recommends that protein consumption is kept to a minimum. While fat consumption must be high, you only need to eat just enough protein to keep your body in good condition. But what is so wrong with eating a lot of protein while following a Ketogenic diet?

Watch your protein intake carefully when on a Ketogenic diet

The first problem presents itself in the form of gluconeogenesis, which we talked about in Chapter 4. Let's say that you sit down to enjoy a large steak lunch. As you eat all that meat, your body will begin to convert the protein into glucose through the process called gluconeogenesis. In fact, for every 100 grams of protein that you consume, 56 grams will be turned into glucose. A few hours after your delicious meal, your blood glucose levels will spike, and your body will burn glucose instead of fat to produce energy. Then you will experience a significant drop in energy levels. Clearly, this goes against everything a Ketogenic diet is supposed to achieve.

The second problem presents itself in the form of insulin. Eating too much protein triggers an increase in insulin levels, and this prevents fat from being broken down. In other words, you will not be able to achieve ketosis.

People who are athletic may worry about losing muscle tone if they don't eat a lot of protein, but as was explained in chapter seven, you can actually gain muscle while under ketosis. In fact, during ketosis, your body actually does its best to preserve muscle.

For the average person following a Ketogenic diet, the recommended range of protein intake is 1.5 to 1.7 grams per kilogram of body weight. For people who are athletic and very active, 2 grams per kilogram of bodyweight will do.

Mistake #8: Failing to Get Adequate Exercise

This mistake is tied into the misconception that ketosis will leave you too weak to engage in any meaningful exercise. This is simply not true. One of the major benefits of a Ketogenic diet is significant long-term weight loss. If your goal is to lose some weight and keep it off, you must combine your Ketogenic lifestyle with some form of exercise.

A person who follows a Ketogenic diet without engaging in exercise will experience slower loss of body fat and fewer health benefits compared to another who works out while under ketosis. Assuming that these two people are friends and meet up after a while, the one who doesn't exercise may wonder what they are doing wrong, since they will notice that their friend has lost weight a lot faster. This explains why some people believe that a Ketogenic diet cannot work for them.

Don't just sit around. Add some exercise to your Ketogenic diet.

On its own, exercise provides immense benefits such as increased muscle growth, stronger bones, increased lung capacity, reduced stress levels, enhanced moods, and prevention of diabetes and heart disease. As you can see, the benefits of the Ketogenic diet and exercise are complementary, regardless of the goals you have set.

If you want to know which types of exercise will work best for you, please refer to Chapter 7, where we talked about the different styles of exercises.

Chapter Summary

Here are the key points of the chapter that you need to remember:

- Eating fatty foods alone will not make you overweight. It is when you combine a high-fat diet with excessive consumption of carbohydrates that you gain weight and become obese.

- Ketoacidosis is not the same thing as ketosis. The only people who should worry about developing ketoacidosis while following a Ketogenic diet are Type 1 diabetes patients. Always consult your physician before going on any kind of diet.

- Keto-adaptation is a difficult process that you need to go through slowly. Do not start consuming a lot of fats without giving your body time to adapt. Transition gradually by eating small snacks that contain a lot of fats.

- Ensure that you drink enough water and take enough minerals and vitamins. A lot of electrolytes are excreted during the initial phase of ketosis, and these need to be replenished.

- Restrict net carbs and not total carbs. This will ensure that you get enough fibre.

- Avoid packaged Ketogenic meals as these may contain hidden starches and sugars. Learn to cook or prepare your own meals using real and whole ingredients.

- Failing to eat a lot of fat while on a Ketogenic diet will negate all the benefits that your body is supposed to receive.

- Avoid eating the wrong kinds of fats such as trans fats and partially hydrogenated oils, which are found in most fast foods and store-bought snacks. Go for good fats like monounsaturated and unsaturated fats.

- Eating too much protein triggers gluconeogenesis and insulin production. This interferes with the breakdown of fat.

- You can still exercise even when on a Ketogenic diet. You will feel very weak at first, but once your body adapts, you will experience greater energy levels than before.

In the next chapter, you will learn some of the reasons why you may fail to achieve a state of ketosis.

Chapter Nine: Reasons Why You Are Not in Ketosis

In this chapter, you will learn why some people have trouble achieving ketosis. There are certain factors that have an impact on your blood ketone levels. It is important to know what these factors are so that you don't end up feeling frustrated when you don't see the results you were expecting. All you have to do is pay attention to your body and follow the correct procedures.

Reason #1: Eating More Carbs than Required

The first reason is pretty obvious, but it is also the most common reason for failing to achieve ketosis. It is important that the moment you start a Ketogenic diet, you set a maximum amount of carbs that you can consume to get into ketosis. The recommended maximum is 50 grams a day, but that doesn't mean you should stick to the upper limit from the start.

You will be better off if you start much lower, say, at about 25 to 30 grams of carbs daily. This will help your body adapt to the new energy source much faster and you will be able to produce ketones for fuel. You need to know your carb range so that you do not end up playing a guessing game. It is easy to assume that you are eating the right amount of carbs, yet your ketone levels could be telling a whole different story.

Don't make assumptions about your ideal carb range. Use an app!

Another thing to watch out for is "hidden" carbs. You need to know the difference between the carb sources to avoid, moderate, and consume. Foods like grains and root vegetables are clearly to be avoided. However, there are some that are allowed but only in moderation, for example, tomatoes, potatoes, and carrots. Blueberries and apples may be allowed, but if you eat too many of them you may exceed your carb limit. You need to keep track of not only the types but also the quantities of carbs you consume.

Reason #2: Too Much Exercise

If you were to test your ketone levels after engaging in strenuous exercise, you would discover that they usually spike about one to two hours later. This is attributed to the increased rate at which fat is broken down into fatty acids. In other words, exercise is great for ketosis.

On the other hand, if you exercise too much, you will reverse the gains you have made. Excessive exercising causes the body to undergo great physical stress, and this triggers the release of a hormone known as *cortisol*. Under normal situations, cortisol is supposed to control inflammation and stress by triggering an immune system response.

131

However, in this case, an increase in cortisol leads to the breakdown of muscle. Cortisol breaks down protein into amino acids that can then be used to create glucose for energy. Do you remember the process of gluconeogenesis we described earlier? This process inhibits ketosis and prevents fats from being the main source of energy.

Exercise is great for ketosis but don't overdo it

This means that you may be eating the right proportions of macronutrients but your excess enthusiasm in the gym may be hindering your ketosis. Make sure that you keep your workouts moderate and don't overdo it.

Reason #3: Time of Day

If your body is already keto-adapted, you should know that blood ketone levels are usually lowest right after you wake up. Your levels tend to rise gradually as the day goes by. This means that you need to find the right time to measure your ketone levels. You could be in a state of ketosis but because you are measuring your blood ketone levels at an inappropriate time of the day, you aren't getting the right readings.

The solution is to identify an appropriate time when your ketone levels are stable. Then make sure that you are consistent with the time of day that you measure your ketosis. Find a time that works for you and stick with it.

Reason #4: Too Much Mental Stress

Though there are times when mental stress is unavoidable, you should know that elevated stress levels will not help you stay in ketosis. This is due to the production of cortisol, which when produced constantly throughout the day for long periods of time can inhibit ketosis.

Avoid too much mental stress to stay in ketosis

Apart from breaking down protein into blood glucose, cortisol also increases your appetite. This is why whenever someone feels stressed out, they quickly think about grabbing some sort of sugary snack. Stress will flood your body with sugar and tempt you to eat more carbs, and these are two factors that are anti-ketogenic.

If you want to achieve and sustain ketosis, you need to find ways of dealing with daily stressors. Find an activity that calms you down and relaxes your mind, otherwise, you may do everything right with your diet but still fail to achieve ketosis.

Reason #5: Lack of Sleep

We all need about seven to eight hours of sleep to ensure that our body performs at an optimal level. However, not getting enough rest can actually hinder you from getting into a state of ketosis. The main cause of the problem, as described before, is the cortisol hormone. Lack of sleep increases your cortisol levels, and even if you are strictly abiding by the recommended carb intake, you will still fail to achieve ketosis.

Sleep is vital for balancing cortisol production

Getting enough sleep is very important, not just for ketosis but for your health in general. If you are not achieving ketosis, then maybe you need to check whether your sleep is the cause of the problem. Try to figure out the minimum amount of sleep that you need per night to keep your cortisol levels stable.

Chapter Summary

Here are the key points of the chapter you need to remember:

- Though you may be following all the right dietary guidelines of a Ketogenic diet, there are some factors that may be preventing you from achieving a state of ketosis.

- You need to watch out for the number of grams of carbs you are consuming. Though 50 grams is the limit, start with a lower amount and keep an eye out for hidden carbs.

- Indulging in too much exercise, failing to get enough sleep, and too much mental stress levels all result in elevated cortisol levels. Cortisol hinders ketosis by breaking down protein to produce blood glucose while also increasing your appetite. Avoid these pitfalls at all cost.

- Be consistent with the time of day that you check your blood ketone levels to avoid inaccurate readings. Ketone levels are usually lowest in the morning, so measure your levels when they are most stable.

In the next chapter, you will learn about the evolution of ketones, and how new research into exogenous ketones is leading to fantastic insights.

Chapter Ten: Exogenous Ketones

In this chapter, you will learn about the evolution of the Ketogenic diet and some of the emerging areas of research involving ketone supplements. The idea of using a low-carb diet to improve health is not new, and we will take a short trip through history to see just how far this concept has come. Exogenous ketones are now a reality and you will learn some of the different types of ketone supplements and their benefits.

In the Beginning

The low-carb diet has come a long way from when it was first conceived in the mid-1800s. A French politician and lawyer was the first person to discover that starches and sugars were responsible for making people obese.

A few years later, William Banting, an English undertaker who had tried everything to lose weight, was advised by his doctor to limit his carbohydrate consumption. Banting was a five-foot-five man who weighed 202 pounds before the diet. He was literally spherical in shape! However, after cutting out beer, bread, milk, potatoes, and sugar from his life, he experienced a remarkable transformation. He lost almost 50 pounds in less than a year.

Later on, people like Bernarr Macfadden would turn society's attention toward the benefits of fasting as a cure for any disease. In the 1920's, Dr Hugh Conklin used fasting as a way to treat epileptic patients and stop their seizures without using drugs. His fellow doctors rejected his claims despite the overwhelming evidence, simply because Conklin himself could not explain why fasting produced such beneficial results in his epileptic patients.

136

In 1921, Dr Rollin Woodyatt began testing the theory that when a diabetic person eats more fat and limits their carbohydrate consumption, insulin would not be produced to manage glucose and fat would be used as fuel. He discovered that the blood of healthy test subjects also contained acetone and beta-hydroxybutyrate.

At that same time, Dr Russel Wilder was also researching on whether a patient can eat healthy fats and receive the benefits of fasting without having to go through starvation. He discovered that when fat is metabolised in the body, particles known as ketone bodies are released, and these particles are then used as an energy source. Dr Wilder went on to suggest that these ketones were the reason why Dr. Conklin's patients had recovered from their epileptic seizures.

Dr Wilder proposed that this state of ketosis could still be created without fasting, and he began recommending a diet rich in fats but low in carbs for his patients. This diet is what we refer to as the Ketogenic diet, and today, it is used for more than just controlling epileptic seizures.

Fast forward to the 1940s, when the German physician Hans Krebs began investigating how ketones could boost the metabolic efficiency of body cells. His research showed that ketones could be used to make cells more efficient in how they utilised energy. Scientists then began wondering whether it was possible to receive all the benefits of ketones without having to go through a Ketogenic diet.

It wasn't long before the US military began taking an interest in ketones. In 2004, the US Defence Advanced Research Projects Agency (DARPA) sponsored a competition where scientists were asked to create a "super fuel" that would help US Special Forces to perform better in combat. This ultimately led to the creation of a *ketone ester*, which is a food that has been approved by the FDA (Food and Drug Administration).

Exogenous Ketones

Exogenous ketones are ketones that are not produced in the body. They are created in a lab and usually taken in form of oral supplements. Maintaining ketosis at all times is not something that everyone can do easily. Therefore, exogenous ketones provide your body with extra ketones even when you are not in ketosis. This can come in handy for beginners who are transitioning into ketosis as well as athletes who need a quick energy boost before a workout.

So far, we have learned of three types of endogenous ketones that are produced by the body: acetoacetate (AcAc), beta-hydroxybutyrate (BHB), and acetone. However, exogenous ketone supplements only contain BHB because the body is able to utilise it most efficiently.

The three types of exogenous ketones include esters, salts, and oils.

Ketone Esters

Ketone esters are made from raw BHB with no other compound bound to it. This helps the body utilise the ketones more quickly. The problem with ketone esters is that they are very expensive and taste like jet fuel. This is why they are mostly used in research rather than for commercial purposes.

Ketone Salts

These are formed by binding ketones to a calcium, magnesium, sodium, or potassium salt. The salts help to boost the absorption rate of the ketones. They are also known as *Ketone Mineral Salts* or *BHB Mineral Salts*. This type of ketone supplement is the most recommended for average consumers, and all the ketone supplements you find in the market today are ketone salts.

Ketone Oil

Unlike the first two supplements, ketone oils do not provide a direct path to increased ketone levels. Ketone oils must first be broken down before the body can use them to produce energy. This means that though they provide a quick energy boost compared to fatty foods, they work much slower than ketone esters and salts. Ketone oils also aren't as effective as esters and salts in raising your ketone levels. Examples of ketone oils include MCT oil powder and coconut oils.

Chapter Summary

Here are the key points of the chapter that you need to remember:

- The low-carb diet was first conceived in the mid-1800s when a French lawyer discovered that carbs were making people obese.

- In the 1920's, Dr Conklin used fasting to treat epileptic patients but was unable to explain why his technique worked.

- In 1921, Dr Wilder discovered that ketones were responsible for the successful treatment of epilepsy when patients were given a high-fat, low-carb diet. He recommended the first Ketogenic diet.

- Research would later show that ketones can boost metabolic efficiency in cells, and the US military looked into the possibility of creating a "super fuel" to help soldiers perform better in combat. This research led to the creation of exogenous ketones.

- Exogenous ketones are ketones made in a lab and taken as oral supplements. They are made from BHB because it is most readily used by the body.

- Ketone esters are made from raw BHB. They are expensive and taste awful, which is why they are mainly used for research only.

- Ketone salts are formed by binding a ketone to mineral salts. They are the most common type of ketone supplement in the market.

- Ketone oil supplements such as MCT oil powder and coconut oils are more effective than consuming fatty foods but don't work as well as ketone esters and salts.

Final Words

You have come to the end of the book, "The *Ketogenic Diet Explained.*" If you did not have any idea what the Ketogenic diet is about, I'm sure your understanding is now much improved. This book has provided you with the basic concepts, techniques, and strategies that you need to begin following a Ketogenic diet. There is much more information to learn, but what you have learned here is more than enough to get you started. Take the knowledge imparted in this book and start your Ketogenic diet one step at a time.

One of the main hindrances that new dieters have is the fact that there are so many misconceptions, myths, and outright lies being peddled about the Ketogenic diet. However, now that you have a book to guide you along the way, you are better placed to differentiate truth from fallacy.

You know now how ketone bodies and ketosis work in your body to boost your health. All the biochemical processes of ketosis have been explained in an easy-to-understand manner. You have also learned what a keto-adapted lifestyle looks like so that you won't be taken by surprise when you experience certain uncommon side effects. Things may get a bit difficult in the initial phases but keep your eyes fixed on the benefits of ketosis. Whatever your goals are – general health, weight loss, improved athletic performance, muscle growth, and treatment of disease – a Ketogenic diet will help you get to where you are going.

Use the tips offered here to ensure that you live a sustainable Ketogenic lifestyle that will bear positive results. Most beginners struggle with knowing which foods to eat and which ones to avoid, but the lists provided in this book are extremely comprehensive. You should now be confident enough to even go out and shop for your first Ketogenic meal. You probably can't wait to try out some of those delectable recipes that can be found in chapter six!

Living a Ketogenic lifestyle can be a rewarding experience. However, the easy part has now come to an end. Buying a book and having knowledge in your head won't do you any good if you don't take action. If you want to benefit from what you have learned in this book, make the decision to start following a Ketogenic diet.

I am honoured that you took the time to read this book. It was a pleasure for me to explain to you some of the important aspects of the Ketogenic diet. I hope you enjoyed reading and learning from this guide.

Thank you and good luck!

The Clever Ketogenic Meal Plan

Ease Into The Keto Lifestyle With Healthy, Practical And Easy To Prep Meal Plans

Charlotte Melhoff

Introduction

Welcome to my book, *The Clever Ketogenic Meal Plan*. Firstly, I'd like to thank you for purchasing my book. Secondly, congratulations! You have taken the first step into the world of keto dieting.

The thing to remember about keto dieting is that it is not just a diet, but an entire lifestyle. It forces you to rethink food and challenge your relationship with carbs and fats unlike any other diet. Contrary to what we are used to with dieting – fats are bad and we have to avoid them at all costs – this diet embraces fats. In fact, 75% of your calorie intake on the keto diet is pure, healthy, good fat. Sounds strange? Maybe. But it really works, and this book will show you exactly how.

The common misconception of fat is that it makes you gain weight. However, this is too simplistic of an idea. Bad fats will cause all sorts of health problems. Carbohydrates will help you gain weight. Good fats on the other hand, like the ones found in avocados, nuts, and salmon, can help you lose weight as they help turn your body into a fat-burning machine. I will explain exactly how this works throughout this book.

Image credit: Africa Studio

Keto dieting has several benefits. Not only does it help to control blood sugar levels in diabetics and lessen seizures in epileptics (the diet's original purpose was to offer relief for this condition and it is still widely recommended for this purpose), it also helps control your appetite, gives you steady energy throughout the day, and helps you lose weight.

This book provides you with four weeks' worth of meal plans tried and tested by me. They helped me lose weight and boost my energy levels, and completely eliminated those midday slumps of fatigue that I used to suffer from. The meal plans are easy to follow and you can find the recipes at the end of the book. I also explain the concept of the keto diet, how you can adapt it to your lifestyle choices or circumstances – such as if you work out or if you have allergies – and how you can stick to the diet easily without committing the most common mistakes of the keto diet.

My aim with this book is to cut through all the information out there about keto dieting and provide you with an honest resource of how it works, what to expect, and all the good and bad points of the keto diet. I hope you feel inspired to try it and enjoy the meal plans as much as I do.

So, without further ado, let's begin by casting all doubts aside. What is the keto diet? You'll find out in Chapter One.

Chapter One: What Is The Ketogenic Diet?

In this chapter, we will look at what the ketogenic diet is and what it does.

The ketogenic diet is a low-carb and high-fat diet. Before we go into more details about that, let's take a look at how our body processes carbohydrates.

When you eat carbohydrates, the body converts it into glucose. Glucose is one of the easiest energy sources for your body to use, and as a result, your body will prefer to use glucose above any other source. The body also produces insulin, which is needed to help process the glucose and feed it into the bloodstream.

What this means is that when you eat carbohydrates, the body uses glucose as the main energy source and ignores the fats. As a result, the fat is stored. The ketogenic diet – sometimes known as the keto diet – focuses on changing the way the body uses energy to switch the energy source from glucose to fat.

The clue behind how the keto diet works is in the name. The term 'keto' comes from the small molecules known as 'ketones' which the body produces as an alternative fuel. The body only makes this energy source when glucose is in low supply and it is made in the liver from fat. The only way to get the body to make ketone is to eat very little carbohydrates and a limited amount of proteins, as excess proteins can also be made into glucose. What all this means is that when the body is producing ketone, it is burning fat instead of carbohydrates, which is an obvious advantage for those looking to lose fat from their bodies.

So why does the body produce ketone in the first place? The brain needs constant energy to function and it can only run on two main sources of energy – glucose and ketone. As a form of protection, if the body doesn't have access to carbs and so can't produce glucose, it will produce ketone instead to keep the brain well-fed. The ketogenic diet forces the body to switch to a state of making its fuel supply come completely from fat.

Where Did The Idea For The Ketogenic Diet Come From?

Interestingly, the ketogenic diet was originally made to help treat epilepsy and not as a diet for weight loss.

In medicine, the keto diet has proved particularly effective in controlling epilepsy in children. As it forces the body to use fats as an energy source rather than carbohydrates, the body has a higher level of ketone bodies in the blood. This increase in ketone molecules has been strongly linked to a reduction in the number of epileptic seizures. In one study, almost half of the participant children with epilepsy found the frequency of their epileptic seizures reduced by half when following the keto diet. Although most of the evidence indicates the effectiveness of the diet in controlling epilepsy in children, there is some evidence that it can help adults with epilepsy, too.

What Happens When Your Body Starts Producing Ketone Instead Of Glucose?

When your body switches to making ketone as an energy source instead of glucose, it is considered to be in a state of ketosis, which is the technical way of saying your body is converting fat into ketone.

It is a natural process for the body and evolved as a survival mechanism for when food supplies are low. It is a different kind of metabolic state than the one in which the body is fed plenty of carbohydrates. You may have heard of people incorporating fasting into their diets, which is another way of moving your body into a state of ketosis. The keto diet doesn't include fasting, but provides the same benefit as fasting provides – inducing weight loss through burning fat rather than carbs. Instead of depriving the body of calories, however, the keto diet simply starves the body of carbohydrates.

Like with any change, you need to get used to the difference. However, the body is a remarkable force of nature and can, eventually, happily adapt to a new metabolic state. There are many advantages to having higher levels of ketone.

The Advantages Of A Ketogenic Diet

Let's take a look at some of the key advantages of a low-carb diet, as with the ketogenic diet. Although weight loss is a key benefit, it isn't the only one. Keto dieting comes with several other benefits that make it a good diet for health purposes, even for those not looking to lose weight and even for those looking to gain weight. The weight loss aspect can be modified when calculating the number of calories you need per day, which we'll look at in the next chapter.

☐   Eating low-carb actually reduces your appetite, which is vital in dieting. One of the main reasons why dieting gets a bad name is that it is commonly associated with feelings of deprivation and, most of all, hunger, which ultimately leads to failure. Proteins and fats keep you full for longer. Not only that, but those that eat fewer carbs and fill up on proteins and fats tend to consume fewer calories in the long run.

☐   Reducing your carb intake is one of the most effective ways to lose weight and studies continue to show that a low-carb diet has a higher rate of weight loss than a low-fat diet. In the initial stages, most of the weight loss is water retention due to the lower insulin levels in the blood, which leads to the kidneys eliminating excess sodium. After this, the lack of carbs makes the body start to burn fat for energy rather than create glucose, which helps create a sustainable approach to weight loss.

☐   It is a good diet for people with diabetes to follow. The ketogenic diet helps to not only lower blood sugar levels, but to stabilise them, too. The macronutrient that increases blood sugar levels the most is the carbohydrate. By eating very few carbs, blood sugar level spikes are reduced. Studies have shown that the main advantage to this is that improvements in blood sugar levels that are maintained for several years can reduce the risks associated with diabetes. Studies have also shown that ketogenic diets can reduce the dependence some diabetics have on their medication for diabetes. Of course, it is always advisable to speak with your doctor about this and to monitor your condition under your doctor's guidance.

☐   Low-carb diets are highly effective at burning the fat stored around your middle area. This kind of fat in the abdominal area is known as visceral fat and is harmful for the health due to the fact it often gets stored around the organs. Low-carb diets burn a higher proportion of visceral fat than low-fat diets.

☐ Eating a low-carb diet can reduce the triglyceride to HDL ratio. What does that mean? First of all, triglycerides are fat molecules whose numbers are increased in the bloodstream after eating carbohydrates, especially fructose. High levels of triglycerides are linked to heart disease. HDL is high-density lipoprotein and its job is to carry fat molecules and cholesterol away from the body and straight to the liver. From there, it can be used or simply moved to waste. HDL is also known as the 'good' cholesterol, which is quite misleading, as it isn't a cholesterol, it just carries cholesterol. However, it is good and you need it. High levels of HDL in your bloodstream mean a lower risk of heart disease. Eating fat increases HDL and a low-carb diet tends to be high in fat. This is where the triglyceride to HDL ratio comes in. The higher the ratio – where your triglyceride levels are high and the HDL levels are low – the higher the risk of heart disease. By improving this, which you can through a low-carb diet, you reduce this risk.

☐ Low-carb diets, especially ketogenic diets, are known to relieve the symptoms of epilepsy. There is also emerging evidence that keto diet may be effective with other neurological disorders, including sleep disorders, bipolar disorders, autism, headaches, brain cancer, and neurogenerative diseases.

The disadvantages of the ketogenic diet are mostly associated with its initial stages, which can be hard to adapt to, especially if you are used to eating high levels of carbohydrates. There are also situations, such as with high-performance athletes, where having ketone as the primary source of energy may not be sufficient. There are ways of adapting this and we will take a look at the challenges and how you can adapt the ketogenic diet to suit your needs over the next few chapters.

First though, let's take a look at how many carbs, fats, and proteins you can eat on the keto diet, which we'll see in the next chapter.

Chapter Summary:

In this chapter, we discovered what the ketogenic diet is and how it can be a healthy dietary lifestyle for the body.

- The ketogenic diet is a low-carb, high-fat, and moderate levels of protein diet. It may feel counter-intuitive, but the high levels of fat and low levels of carbs is actually highly effective for weight loss, especially around the abdomen.

- Eating a low-carb and high-fat diet forces the body to switch into a state of ketosis, which is when the body stops using glucose as its primary source of energy and starts converting fat into ketone as the main energy source.

- There are several advantages of following the ketone diet, including more effective weight loss than a low-fat diet, reduced risk of heart disease, reduction in epileptic seizures, and increased control of blood sugar levels in those with diabetes.

In the next chapter, we will look in more detail at the quantities of food you can eat and how to calculate your keto daily allowance.

Chapter Two: Calculating Your Dietary Intake On A Keto Diet

In this chapter, we will look at the percentages and amounts of fats, carbs, and proteins that you need to eat. We will also look at how you can calculate how many grams of each of the macronutrients you need to remain in a state of ketosis.

Before knowing what you can and can't eat on the keto diet, you should know what quantities of macronutrients (that's your fats, proteins, and carbohydrates) you can eat. Your daily food intake should come from the following percentages:

☐ 75% of your food consumption per day should come from fat.

☐ 20% of your food consumption per day should come from protein.

☐ 5% of your food consumption per day should come from carbohydrates.

This can be adapted to suit your needs – if you exercise heavily, for example – but this is the general ratio of the ketogenic diet.

So, how do you calculate your daily consumption?

This is broken down into four parts.

☐ **Step One:** Calculate your BMR, otherwise known as your Basic Metabolic Rate. This is how much energy your body needs to survive and perform its essential bodily functions, such as pumping blood, breathing, and digesting food.

☐ **Step Two:** Calculate how many extra calories you need to perform your daily exercise routine or any physical exercise that you do. This is known as your TDEE, or Total Daily Energy Expenditure, and includes all the calories you need per day.

☐ **Step Three:** You need to decide whether you want to gain weight, maintain your weight, or lose weight. If you want to lose weight, for example, you will have a calorie deficit diet where you consume fewer calories than you use. If you want to maintain your weight, you eat the right number of calories for what you use. If you want to gain weight, you eat more calories than you burn.

☐ **Step Four**: Allocate your calories per day to the keto ratios of proteins, carbs, and fats we saw above.

Let's calculate your daily consumption of proteins, carbs, and fats.

Step One: Calculate Your BMR

We will use the Mifflin-St Jeor formula to calculate BMR, as it is considered the most accurate. This is the manual method for doing it, although if you search online, there are calculators that can do this for you.

There is a slight difference between calculating the BMR between men and women.

☐ For men, the formula is:
10 x weight (kilograms) + 6.25 x height (centimetres) – 5 x age (years) + 5

☐ For women, the formula is:
10 x weight (kilograms) + 6.25 x height (centimetres) – 5 x age (years) – 161

Make sure you do this calculation as a whole equation rather than calculating part by part. Type all the numbers and actions in the sequence above before pressing 'equals'.

Let's see an example:

If we have a man that is 1.9 metres tall, weighs 88kgs, and is 32 years old, we would calculate his BMR in the following way:

10 x 88 + 6.25 x 190 – 5 x 32 + 5 = 1,853 calories.

So, that means he needs 1,853 calories per day to function normally, without considering any exercise.

Let's do the same for a woman. Let's say we have a woman who is 1.7 metres tall, weighs 62 kg, and is 45 years old. To get her BMR, we would do the following:

10 x 62 + 6.25 x 170 -5 x 45 – 161 = 1,297 calories.

So, this woman needs 1,297 calories per day to keep her body healthy.

From the BMR, we can calculate TDEE.

Step Two: Calculate Your TDEE

To calculate your TDEE, you need to factor in the calories you require to perform your daily or weekly physical activity. To do this, we need to use activity level multipliers, which are numbers that represent the level of exercise you do. Here is the activity level multiplier guide:

1.2 – Sedentary, or little to no exercise per week.

1.38 – Light exercise. About one to three hours per week.

1.55 – Moderate exercise. Between four and six hours per week.

1.73 – Hard exercise. Between seven or more hours per week of exercise on top of a physical job.

1.9 – Extremely active. This includes multi-training workouts plus two or more workouts per day. This is a professional athlete level, especially endurance sports.

These numbers reflect all physical activity you do, including weight lifting, physical labor, and cardio training. If you are not sure between two levels, select a number in between each category for a more appropriate estimate. It's important to carefully consider your activity level multiplier. Even bodybuilders are often in the moderate category, and the majority of non-sporty people are in the moderate category or less.

Let's continue with an example. This calculation is pretty straight forward.

The guy we saw earlier had a BMR of 1,853 calories. Let's suppose he works as a software developer and works out between three to four times a week at the gym. We can say that he fits into the light category. So, to calculate his TDEE, we do the following:

1,853 x 1.38 = 2,557 calories.

In other words, he needs 2,557 calories per day to function healthily and to perform his regular exercise.

The woman had a BMR of 1,297 calories per day. Let's say she works out five times a week, plays tennis once a week, swims twice a week, and regularly goes hiking. She also works as an account manager, so she is regularly on her feet moving between meetings. She fits into the moderate category. To calculate her TDEE, we need to do the following equation.

1,297 x 1.55 = 2,010 calories.

So, she needs 2,010 calories per day to function normally and to do the exercise she does per week.

The next step in calculating how many calories you need to get from proteins, carbs, and fats in the keto diet is to determine whether you want a calorie deficit, calorie sustained, or calorie surplus.

Step Three: Adjust Calorie Intake For Weight Control

You need to adjust your TDEE to be able to control your weight the way you want.

☐ If you want to lose weight, you should have a calorie deficit of 20%. Lower than this will reduce the margin of error; higher will be hard to sustain and will make you feel   hungry.

☐ To gain weight, you need a calorie surplus of 20%.

☐ To sustain your weight as it is right now, simply use your TDEE as calculated in step two and jump straight to step four.

For example, the woman we saw earlier had a TDEE of 2,010 calories. If she wants to lose weight, she would need to do the following calculation to get the calories per day with a 20% reduction.

2,010 – (2,010 x 0.2) = 1,608 calories per day.

If she wanted to gain weight, she needs to do the following to include an additional 20%.

2,010 + (2,010 x 0.2) = 2,412 calories per day.

These numbers aren't set in stone, and as your weight, exercise routine, or goals change, you can recalculate and adjust the above numbers.

Step Four: Work Out How Many Macronutrients You Need

Now, we can finally work out how many carbs, fats, and proteins you need to follow the ketogenic diet while meeting your body's needs.

Carbohydrates, proteins, and fats are referred to as macronutrients and are nutrients that supply our bodies with energy. They are the opposite of micronutrients, which are vitamins and minerals, but right now, we will just pay attention to macros.

To calculate how many macros you need, it's good to know both how many calories you can eat of proteins, carbs, and fats and how many grams that is equivalent to. Here's how you can calculate that:

To make it easy, let's say that your TDEE, which has already factored in your weight loss goals, is 2,000 calories per day.

To do the ketogenic diet and remain in a state of ketosis, 5% of your daily calories needs to be carbs, 20% needs to be proteins, and 75% needs to be fats.

For carbs: 2,000 x 0.05 = 100 calories per day needs to be carbs.

What is that in grams? Well, there are 4 calories in a gram of carbohydrates. So, divide the calories for your daily carbs by four to get the quantity of grams.

This would be: 100 / 4 = 25 grams of carbs per day.

In the beginning, you shouldn't eat more than 50 grams per day, so if your calculation gives you more than 50 grams, round it down to 50.

For proteins: 2,000 x 0.2 = 400 calories per day should be proteins.

What is that in grams? Like carbs, there are 4 calories in a gram of protein. So, divide the calories for your daily proteins by four to get the quantity of grams.

This would be: 400 / 4 = 100 grams of proteins per day.

For fats. 2,000 x 0.75 = 1,520 calories per day needs to be fats.

What is that in grams? Fats have 9 calories per gram. So, divide the number of calories for your daily fat allowance by nine to get the quantity of grams.

This would be: 1,520 / 9 = 169 grams of fat per day.

And that's it! That is how you calculate how much of each macronutrient you should be eating per day. So, now that you know exactly how much protein, carbs, and fats you should be eating, what kind of food can you actually eat? That's what we will look at in the next chapter.

Chapter Summary:

In this chapter, we looked at how to calculate exactly how much you should be eating when on a ketogenic diet. This is important to ensure that your body remains in a state of ketosis and burns fat for energy instead of carbs.

- To follow a ketogenic diet, you need to make sure you daily consumption of food is broken down into 5% carbohydrates, 20% proteins, and 75% fats.

- To know exactly how many calories you need per day and how to allocate these into the three main macronutrient groups, you need to follow four steps. First, calculate your BMR. Next, calculate your TDEE, which factors in the exercise you do each week. Then, adjust your calorie intake to represent your weight goals. Finally, divide the overall daily calories into the ketogenic diet ratios.

In the next chapter, we will look at which foods you can eat on ketogenic diet.

Chapter Three: Food You Can Eat On The Ketogenic Diet

In this chapter, we will look at the different foods you can eat on the ketogenic diet. We will also look at which foods to avoid.

One of the key points to make about the keto diet is that while you should eat very low quantities of carbs, you should also make sure you eat 'real' food. In other words, food with natural ingredients and not processed. This is simply a good food decision to ensure you give your body the best possible fuel it can get.

The following food groups are accepted on the keto diet. Not only will they provide you with the nutrients and vitamins you need to stay healthy, they will also help you stick to the 5% carbs restriction.

☐ Fats and oils. These will make up a large part of your keto diet. The best sources of fats and oils are natural food products such as meat (preferably organic) and nuts. You can also cook or flavor food with a mix of saturated and monounsaturated fats such as olive oil, coconut oil, and pure organic butter.

Image credit: Maria Uspenskaya

☐ Protein. The easiest sources of protein are meat and fish, although there are other foods that are a source of protein, too. If you eat meat, then organic, grass-fed meat is always the best choice whenever possible. Proteins should be eaten in a moderate quantity and shouldn't exceed 20% of the total daily intake of food.

Image credit: Tanya Sid

☐ Vegetables. Leafy, green items such as lettuce, kale, and broccoli are great vegetables to stick to. Other vegetables, such as beetroot, onions, and parsnips can also be eaten in moderation.

Image credit: Svetlana Lukienko

☐ Dairy. As dairy has high levels of fat, it is a good option to eat. However, some dairy is better than others. You should stick to full-fat items and harder cheeses, as these have fewer carbs than soft cheeses.

Image credit: margouillat photo

☐ Nuts and seeds. Nuts and seeds are great to add extra texture and taste to salads and sauces. They can turn a simple meal into something really tasty. The best kinds of nuts and seeds to eat are the fatty ones, such as almonds, sunflower seeds, macadamias, Brazil nuts, and flaxseeds.

Image credit: Krysztof Slusarczyk

☐ Drinks. Water is the best beverage you can drink. You can flavor it with a squeeze of lemon, lime, ginger, garlic, or any other natural flavorings. Alcohol is best avoided, especially drinks such as beer and cocktails which have high levels of carbs and sugar.

Image credit: Krzysztof Slusarczyk

That's a brief summary of the food groups you can eat. In a later chapter, we will look at meal plans that you can easily follow. For now, we will look in greater detail at the different food groups, so that, if you want, you can create your own meal plans.

The Ideal Food Groups For The Ketogenic Diet

Fats And Oils

Fats and oils come with a negative image and are often associated with weight gain, heart disease, and other health complications. However, there are several types of fats. Some are vital for the body to function correctly, whereas others can cause health issues. It is important to know which of the different fats you should eat and which ones you should avoid.

☐ Saturated fats. These are good fats and you should eat them on the ketogenic diet. These include butter and coconut oil. You can use these in cooking or to flavor your meal.

☐ Monounsaturated fats. Again, these are a type of fats you can eat. Avocados are a great source of monounsaturated fats, as are olives and almonds.

☐ Polyunsaturated fats. There are two types of polyunsaturated fats. One is good, the other is not. The good type is the naturally-occurring one that is found mostly in meat and fatty fish such as salmon. These are great for your health and you can definitely eat these. The one to avoid is the processed polyunsaturated fats, such as in margarine. It's these that are linked to heart disease. That's why it is always better to eat natural, unprocessed food wherever possible as it becomes easier to avoid the bad kinds of food.

☐ Trans fat. Trans fats are the ones that give fats a bad name. These are best to avoid at all costs, as they don't provide any kind of nutrients or benefits for the body and are linked to numerous health problems. These kinds of fats have been hydrogenated to make them last longer. In other words, they have been chemically modified and are no longer natural.

The ones you should try to eat, then, are the saturated and monounsaturated fats as they are the healthiest.

The fats and oils food group will make up about 75% of your calorie intake. The good news is that it's pretty easy to get this quantity into your diet, as there are plenty of options to choose from.

Here are some different fats you can eat on the keto diet.

☐ Fatty fish, such as salmon, tuna, and sardines.

☐ Avocados.

☐ Eggs, especially the yolk, which is a rich source of fats.

☐ Brazil nuts, macadamias, almonds, and sunflower seeds.

☐ Animal fat that isn't trans-fats, such as lard.

☐ Various types of oils, such as avocado, coconut, olive, and macadamia.

☐ Butter, especially pure butter, cocoa butter, and coconut butter.

☐ Vegetable oils, such as soybean, safflower, and flax. Opt for cold-pressed options where possible.

Image credit: Maria Uspenskaya

Fats are a good source of omega-3, which is an essential oil for the body. You can get omega-3 from eating salmon, tuna, sardines, trout, and shellfish. If you don't like fish or have an allergy, take an omega-3 supplement to make sure you get your daily requirement of this essential fatty acid.

Another essential fatty acid is omega-6, which can be found in most nuts, seeds, and oils. Although important for the body, try to avoid snacking on nuts to ensure that you keep the omega levels at normal standards. The great thing about ketogenic diets is that it is easy to get sufficient quantities of omega oils, something that is harder to do on low-fat diets.

Protein

After fats, the next food group that you will be consuming the most is protein. However, it will still make up a small part of your diet at just 20% of all daily calorie intake. When choosing protein-based food to eat, it's best to pick proteins that are fatty. Also, grass-fed and organic meat is always the best bet, as it will probably have fewer quantities of certain types of steroid hormones. The best fatty meats to eat are dark meat and fatty fish.

Be careful when eating proteins, as too much can cause the body to start processing glucose instead of ketone, pushing your body out of a ketogenic state. Keeping an eye on your protein intake will ensure that you don't overconsume on proteins and remain in ketosis.

Here are some proteins that you can consume on the ketogenic diet:

☐ Shellfish. Shellfish have high levels of protein, so eat in moderation. Shellfish you can eat include lobster, mussels, oysters, clams, squid, or crab.

☐ Eggs. You can eat these in any way you want. They have low levels of protein, so it is easier to eat without overconsuming on protein. If you can get them free-range, then even better.

☐ Poultry. This includes meats such as pheasant, duck, chicken, and turkey. Chicken is a source of high levels of protein. Duck and goose are great choices due to their high fat content.

☐ Fish. Fatty fish, such as salmon, sardines, and tuna are the best picks, although take care, as they have high levels of protein too. Other good fishes to eat include cod, flounder, mackerel, snapper, and catfish.

☐ Pork. Pork chops have high levels of protein, so eat them in moderation. Other pork items include ground pork, tenderloin, and ham. Watch out for sausages, as they often contain additional sugars and try to avoid processed ham. Cured ham can also have added sugar and processed ingredients. Bacon has low levels of protein and is high in fat (one of the highest foods on the list, in fact); just make sure to check the ingredients for any added sugar.

☐ Beef. The fattier, the better. Steak, minced beef, and roasted beef are all good options. Stewing beef is a good choice, too, as it's quite fatty.

☐ Other meat. This includes goat, lamb, veal, and venison. All of this is fine to eat.

☐ Organs. For those that like organs, such as kidney, offal, liver, heart, and tongue, these items are certainly on the menu, as they have moderate levels of protein and relatively high fat levels.

☐ Nut butter. Almond and macadamia nut butters are the best you can opt for.

Image credit: dar193o

Vegetables And Fruits

These are an important part of almost any diet and the ketogenic diet is no exception. Just make sure you avoid the ones that have high levels of carbs, such as potatoes.

The best types of vegetable are the ones that are leafy, because they are high in nutrients and very low in carbs, making them a perfect filler for any meal. Interestingly, there isn't much difference in nutritional value between organic or non-organic vegetables, which is a relief for those on a budget. The main benefit of buying organic is that there are fewer pesticides. Also, whether you buy fresh or frozen makes little difference – whatever is more convenient for you.

Below the ground vegetables do have higher levels of carbs than leafy greens, but you can still eat them in moderation. For example, adding onion or chopped beetroot to a soup or salad can add flavor and still keep you in a state of ketosis.

Here are some great vegetables to eat:

- Leafy vegetables: spinach, lettuce, kale, cabbage, cress, Swiss chard, and bok choy.

- Others: Baby Bella mushrooms, green bell peppers, and green beans.

The following you can eat, but try to only eat in moderation when you do eat them:

- Root vegetables: onions, parsnips, garlic, squash, and mushrooms. You can eat these as parts of a soup, of a leafy salad, or to make a simple, small vegetable salad.

174

☐ Berries: raspberries, blackberries, and blueberries. Berries can be eaten in moderation when you want a sweet snack, but be careful, as they have high levels of sugar.

☐ Citrus: lemon, lime, and orange juice. You can use these to flavor meals and add to water.

☐ Nightshades: tomatoes, peppers, and eggplants all fall into this category and make great additions to salads or accompaniments to meals.

What to avoid:

☐ Starchy vegetables and fruits are best avoided. These include potatoes, bananas, and winter squash.

Image credit: Roman Rybaleov

Dairy Products

Dairy products can be consumed on the ketogenic diet, but should be eaten in moderation. Some products contain higher levels of carbs than others, so pay attention to that when making your dairy choices.

Here are some tips for eating dairy:

☐ Eat raw and organic whenever possible. Why? Because processed dairy has much higher levels of carbohydrates than non-processed.

☐ The best kind of dairy is full-fat rather than fat-free or low-fat. It may sound contrary to what you are used to if you have always followed low-fat diets, but high-fat is what you want from your dairy products on the ketogenic diet.

☐ What can you do if you have lactose intolerance? Obviously, this depends on the level of your intolerance. If you are allergic, you should completely avoid any kind of lactose. If you can still have lactose in moderation, then try eating the very hard or aged dairy products, as they have less lactose in them.

☐ You should get most of your calories and nutrients from proteins, vegetables, fats, and oils, but some dairy is totally fine and makes a great extra for meals and snacks.

☐ Dairy offers a quick way to get extra fat into a meal. You can make sauces like a creamy, cheesy sauce for vegetables, add mayonnaise to meat, or add thick cream to coffee. Just take care with the protein content in cheese, as you want to minimise this whenever possible.

Here are some dairy products you can eat:

☐ Greek yogurt. This makes a great breakfast or snack option.

☐ Homemade mayonnaise. Great to add to dressings or sauces.

☐ Hard cheese. These are the best for their low-carb content. They include aged cheddar, parmesan, and Swiss cheese.

☐ Soft cheese. You can eat soft cheese, just be careful with their higher carb content. This includes Brie, blue cheese, and mozzarella.

☐ Whipping cream. Select the full-fat option.

☐ Cheese you can spread is fine in smaller quantities. This includes cream cheese, crème fraiche, mascarpone, cottage cheese, and sour cream.

Image credit: Vlasov Yevhenii

Nuts And Seeds

Nuts and seeds are great extras to include in meals and snacks for extra fat, flavour, and texture. Some types have higher levels of carbs than others, so watch out for that.

Tips for eating nuts and seeds:

- ☐ Avoid peanuts, as they aren't considered a good food in the ketogenic diet.

- ☐ Roasted nuts and seeds are the best to eat, if possible. Also, raw nuts are fine for flavor or texture.

- ☐ Try avoiding snacking on nuts, as this can have a detrimental·effect on weight loss and can increase insulin levels.

- ☐ Plus, in addition to fats, nuts have significant quantities of proteins and carbs. They also have high levels of omega-6 fatty acids. Make sure you eat nuts in moderation.

- ☐ Almond flour is often replaced with sunflower seed flour by those with nut allergies. This is totally fine on the ketogenic diet. Just be careful with the amount you use, as sunflower seed flour has high levels of omega-6 fatty acids.

The best nuts to eat are the one that are high in fats and low in carbs. Here are several types of nuts and their nutrient content, which will help you decide what you should eat on a keto diet.

☐ High in fat, low in carbs: pecans, Brazil nuts, and macadamia nuts.

☐ High in fat, moderate amount of carbs: peanuts, pine nuts, almonds, walnuts, and hazelnuts.

☐ High in fat, but also high in carbs: cashews and pistachios. These two should be avoided completely. Cashews, for example, are very high in carbs – just two handfuls is almost the equivalent of the daily allowance of carbs on the keto diet.

Image credit: Maciej Bled owski

You can use a combination of different flours to make a variety of items that are within the ketogenic diet, such as muffins and pizza bases. Great flours to use that are low in carbs are almond flour, coconut flour, chia seed meal, and flaxseed meal. However, still use in moderation, as some, such as almond flour, are high in protein.

Drinks

Without a doubt, water is the best beverage you can drink on the keto diet. It is recommended to drink eight glasses of water per day, but it is better if you can drink more, as in the beginning stages of ketosis, dehydration is quite common due to the natural diuretic effect. You can drink water freely without any restrictions.

Here is a list of drinks you can and shouldn't drink on the keto diet:

☐ Water. Drink as much as you like. It can be either still or sparkling, whatever your preference.

☐ Coffee. Coffee is part of the morning ritual for many people and that's totally fine. Also, coffee can stimulate weight loss. Stick to a maximum of two coffees per day.

☐ Tea. The best kind of tea you can drink is black or green tea. The latter has been linked to weight loss, too.

☐ Broth. Not only is this a great liquid to quench your thirst, but it is also full of vitamins, helping to give you extra nutrients that you may need.

☐ Milk. The best type of milk to drink is unsweetened coconut or almond milk.

☐ Flavorings. You can add flavorings made with sucralose or stevia to water to make it more pleasant if you don't like drinking water.

☐ Soda. Even diet fizzy drinks are best avoided. They can lead to sugar cravings that are hard to control.

☐ Alcohol. If possible, avoid completely. It can hinder weight loss and lead to cravings. Beer and wine are full of carbs and are not recommended on the keto diet. If you really want to drink something – such as when you are at a social event – stick to neat, hard liquor like pure vodka and ice.

Image credit:Syda Productions

Those are the major food groups that you should think about when you are on the keto diet. Yet, how about when you want to add flavor to a meal? In the next section, we will look at spices, herbs, and sauces that you can use.

Spices And Herbs

Here are some tips for using spices and herbs as part of a keto diet:

☐ Avoid processed condiments, as these make it hard to trace the carbs and sugar. Low-carb condiments may be fine, but some have high levels of sweeteners, which is not good for the keto diet. Stick to natural wherever possible. Many spice mixes have added sugar to them, too.

☐ Many people are surprised to learn that spices have carbs in them, but they do, so use sparingly.

☐ Use sea salt rather than table salt. Why? Table salt is often mixed with a powder form of dextrose, which is best avoided.

Here are some of the best spices and herbs to use:

☐ Salt and pepper. You can use these freely.

☐ Cinnamon. Great to add to coffee if you like that extra taste.

☐ Thyme.

☐ Parsley.

☐ Chili powder.

☐ Cumin.

☐ Basil.

☐ Rosemary.

☐ Cayenne pepper.

☐ Oregano.

Sauces

Here are some tips on how to consume sauces on the keto diet:

☐ The sauces you can eat on the keto diet are listed below. Other than these, it is best to avoid processed sauces, as they often have added sugar.

☐ Some great low-carb, high-fat sauces include anything butter-based, such as garlic butter or a hollandaise sauce.

☐ Whenever you buy pre-made sauces, always check the label beforehand to make sure the sugar content is low.

You can make your own sauces, but if you are one of the many who simply don't have time for this, then the following are absolutely fine to use on the keto diet:

☐ Mustard.

☐ Mayonnaise.

☐ Ketchup with no sugar.

☐ Horseradish.

☐ Chili or hot sauce.

☐ Relish.

☐ Salad dressings, such as Caesar or ranch dressings.

☐ Brown sauce with no sugar.

How about when you want something sweet? Sugar is off the menu, but sweeteners are fine to use. However, this largely depends on the type of sweeteners you consume. Here's some tips for sweeteners:

- Liquid versions are best over powder sweeteners. Powder versions often have ingredients such as dextrose and maltodextrin, which are forms of carbs.

- The best kind of sweeteners you can have are the ones that have a low glycemic index.

The different types of sweeteners that are keto-friendly are:

- Stevia. This is definitely one of the best choices of sweeteners and is also one of the most popular.

- Sucralose. This is another good sugar substitute.

- Erythritol. This is one of the best ones and a mix of stevia and erythritol makes the perfect sweetener. The body doesn't digest erythritol, so none of its carbs are absorbed.

- Other brands. Take care if you use other brands. Check the nutritional content carefully to make sure there isn't a high level of carbs.

We just looked at what you can eat on the keto diet. It's also useful to know exactly what you should avoid. Here are some foods you definitely shouldn't eat on the keto diet.

Foods To Totally Avoid

☐ Grains. Loaded with carbs, any type of grain should be avoided at all costs. This includes whole meal, too, such as corn, rye, wheat, rice, and oats. Also included in this category is quinoa, white potatoes, pasta, crackers, cookies, pizza, and bread. All kind of sugar or sugar-based products – table sugar, ice cream, cakes, soft drinks – are included. However, you can actually make pizza bases with almond flour, for example, which give a similar texture but are much more keto-friendly. So, while the original versions are off the menu, there is room for innovation and creativity to make other keto-options.

☐ Factory-farmed meat. This is especially related to fish and pork, which may be high in omega-6 fatty acids.

☐ Some sweeteners. Some artificial sweeteners are best avoided completely, as they score high on the glycemic index. These include Splenda, Saccharin, and any type with Aspartame.

☐ Processed foods. Any type of processed food is best avoided, as they often contain hidden carbs and sugars.

☐ Any kind of trans-fats. They don't provide any kind of health benefit and are disruptive to the keto diet.

☐ Low-carb products. The low-carb and even zero-carbs products may sound appealing. However, the reality is they may be high in artificial sweeteners, gluten, etc.

☐ Alcohol. Alcohol is really best avoided, especially beer, wine, and cocktails.

☐ Milk. While raw milk in small quantities is okay, just be careful, as it still has a fairly high number of carbs. The issue with milk is that it's hard to digest and may contain hormones. It is better to replace milk in coffee or tea with full-fat cream.

☐ Some fruit. Fruits such as bananas, mangos, and pineapples have high levels of sugar, so are best avoided. Fruits such as grapes or tangerines have high quantities of carbs, so are also off the menu, except for a squeeze of orange juice in water to give it flavor. Fruit juices are high in sugar, even the totally natural ones, so it's better to replace them with water and a slice of lime or lemon. Dried fruits such as raisins or sultanas are high in sugar, so avoid them.

Chapter Summary:

In this chapter, we looked at all the foods you can eat and the foods you should avoid.

- Fats and oils will make up the largest portion of your diet. Try to stick to high-fat, low-carb content as much as possible.

- Proteins will make up the second largest portion of your diet. Choose fatty proteins and be careful not to overconsume proteins, as this can make the body start producing glucose.

- Finally, carbs will make up the smallest amount and will come from foods such as vegetables and from proteins.

- Stick to natural, unprocessed food whenever possible.

- Be careful with fruit. Some is okay, but many fruits contain high levels of sugar.

- Stick to water as your primary drink and try drinking at least eight glasses per day, ideally more. Ketogenic diets naturally make you more dehydrated, especially in the beginning. Avoid alcohol, especially if you are aiming to lose weight.

In the next chapter, we will be looking at the stages of the ketogenic diet, the obstacles and mental challenges you may face, some of the downsides you can expect, and how to overcome these.

Chapter Four: The Different Phases Of The Ketogenic Diet

In this chapter, we will be looking at some of the challenges faced when starting the ketogenic diet. These are the downsides of living a keto lifestyle, but the good news is, these reactions are just in the initial stages. They will pass in a couple or a few weeks.

The ketogenic diet has many health benefits. Not only does it stimulate weight loss, it is also linked to reducing the risk of heart disease and diabetes, protecting against some neurological conditions, and improving general cognitive function.

However, it can be a big change in the beginning for your body to move from using glucose as its primary energy source to using ketone. Also, the different portions of food will take your body some time to get used to, especially if you are used to eating starchy foods with high levels of carbohydrates and sugar. It is not a swift and simple transition, but it is beneficial and any challenges will pass. Here are some of the things you can expect in the initial stages of switching to a ketogenic diet.

☐ **The keto flu.** Many people get what is known as the keto flu in the first few days. As we mentioned before, the ketogenic diet is a natural diuretic and it's easy to become dehydrated in the initial stages. You may also lose essential electrolytes. The lack of electrolytes and dehydration result in flu-like symptoms that can be quite unpleasant. The way to avoid this is to drink plenty of water and make sure you keep your body replenished with electrolytes. You can do this by drinking specific sports drinks that are filled with electrolytes and sweetened with stevia or by drinking natural broth, which is full of nutrients.

☐ **Constipation.** This is a pretty unwelcome initial side effect, but it can happen in the beginning stages. The keto diet means you will be consuming only small amounts of carbs and fiber. If you were already doing this before the diet, then you should be fine, as it will be easier to adapt. However, if you were eating high levels of lots of carbs and fiber prior to starting the keto diet, this change can have an impact on your digestive system and the main adverse effect is constipation. There are some ways of lessening the effects of this. Make sure you drink lots of water and try eating plenty of low carb vegetables throughout the day. Great vegetables to eat include leafy greens and avocados. This may naturally help to keep your digestive system moving as normal. If you are still having issues with constipation, then take a digestive enzyme supplement. The best one to take has the lipase enzyme in it, which helps break down fats.

☐ **Low energy.** It's not a quick and easy task for your body to switch from processing glucose for fuel to converting fat to ketone for energy. There are a lot of metabolic changes at play. This transition period triggers your body to store energy as the changes in metabolism occur. Eventually this will pass, but in the meantime, you may feel weak, tired, fatigued, and have lower levels of cognitive sharpness. Dehydration is a key reason for low energy levels, so make sure you stay hydrated by drinking lots of water and by getting the electrolytes and nutrients that you need. Broth, as mentioned before, is great to replenish nutrients that are commonly lost during ketosis and will help keep headaches and cramps at bay.

☐ **Muscle weakness.** This may happen in the beginning stages, but it will improve, and you should eventually get higher energy levels than before. However, in the beginning, it's good to stick to light exercises and wait until your energy levels are back up to hit any intense training. Another thing you may notice is a longer recovery time from a hard or challenging workout.

☐ **Hypoglycemia.** This is the technical term for low blood sugar levels and can be an issue in the initial phases of the ketogenic diet, especially as the body is in the transition period to ketosis. Symptoms include feeling lightheaded, sweating more than usual, or feeling shaky. If you feel this, you need to relax and drink some fruit juice or eat a few pieces of hard candy.

☐ **Cravings.** Anyone that has tried a diet before will be familiar with the feelings of cravings. When you radically alter your diet, cravings are a common side effect. One great benefit of the keto diet is that it actually reduces your appetite, so you can eat fewer calories and not feel overly hungry. However, you may feel cravings for carbs or sugar, which is normal when you change your diet. Your body is going through a process that can be likened to 'withdrawal' and this can take time to get over. Often, certain foods we eat are not just for fuel, but also have emotional links and are comfort foods. Just be aware of this and know that in time this will change. Make sure you are still eating enough calories in the beginning and reduce them gradually so you can get used to the new foods without feeling hungry, which will help you feel better.

☐ **Changes in temperament.** Feeling moody? Then it's probably because of the keto diet. The digestive system is closely linked to the nervous system and you may have already noticed how your mood changes when you are hungry. For some people, this is a subtle change, but for others, it can be far more significant. Changes to your diet affect hormone production and this will play a huge role in how well you sleep and feel. It's perfectly normal to feel grouchy and moody in the first couple of weeks of your diet and it's important to remember that this will change. It's just your body's way of getting used to the new energy source of ketone. Exercising can lift your mood, so try a gentle walk or yoga in the beginning stages to give you a light, uplifting workout that doesn't put too much stress on your body.

Those are the main issues you can expect in the beginning of changing to a keto diet and these symptoms can last around a month. During this time, you will still notice weight loss, but the other benefits of the ketogenic diet, such as healthy skin and hair and increased energy levels will probably take a couple or so weeks after starting to be noticeable. So, stay strong and keep pushing through the initial stages.

One major issue is that the ketogenic diet is restricting. Cheat days can take you out of ketosis and it can take a couple of days for the body to clear out the glucose stores and go back to converting fat into fuel. You have to be dedicated and committed to the diet.

Low-carb diets may seem hard to follow in the beginning, but it's simply a case of getting used to it. There are also several alternatives to your usual carbs that will make it easier to stick to the keto diet. Here are some tips on overcoming the challenges of a strict, low-carb diet.

☐ Get into the habit of counting your carbs every day. Having something you are accountable for will help you stick to your goals. If you make guesses, you may make mistakes, which will not give you the results you want. Get into the habit of carb counting from the very beginning to get you thinking about carbs and learning what to avoid. It will take time in the beginning, but before you know it, you will understand how many carbs are in what automatically. This will only happen, though, if you put in the effort in the beginning, so make sure you read all labels and know the quantity of carbs you are eating per day. You can calculate exactly how many carbs you should eat using the calculations we covered in Chapter Two.

☐ The keto diet is not just a diet; it's a lifestyle. What this means is that you need to adopt it radically and make it a part of your daily routine. What's the first step to do this? Clear out your kitchen cupboards, fridge, and freezer. Make sure that all the food you have in your kitchen is keto-friendly if possible. This will help you in moments where you want to eat bread or chocolate or anything else that is not on the keto menu. If the food you are craving is there in front of you, it takes a willpower of steel to ignore it. Save yourself the torment by simply not having it in the kitchen in the first place.

☐ Going to restaurants is a whole new ballgame when you are on the ketogenic diet and it requires preparation so you know what you can and can't eat. The first rule is to substitute fries, potatoes, or potato wedges for vegetables. Even if the restaurant has low-carb foods, you won't truly know the sugar content, so it's best to avoid them and stock up on vegetables instead. For breakfast, try ordering eggs and bacon with a coffee and cream for a protein -

based, fat-rich meal. For lunch, chicken or fish with a big green salad is a perfect option. For dinner, meat with vegetables will be keto-friendly. It's fine to order a steak, just make sure it doesn't come with fries. If you can, check the menu online before you go so you know when you can order. Also, avoid drinking alcohol or eating dessert.

☐ What if you're out and about and want a keto-friendly snack? Those random, niggly hunger pangs can test your strength sometimes when it comes to dieting and the best way to overcome them is to be prepared by having snacks on hand. If you fancy something sweet, have a small pot of peanut butter mixed with chopped celery and stevia sweetener. You will barely taste the celery, but it will add a satisfying crunch and texture. The sweetener will make the peanut butter seem like a dessert, but it will not mess up your keto diet and will ward off sweet cravings. Nuts are also a good snack to have on hand, just be careful not to go overboard eating them as they still have high levels of proteins. Another great snack is little cubes of hard cheese or even kale crisps that you can make at home and take out with you.

How To Know If You Are In Ketosis

A few days after starting the ketogenic diet, your body will have used its reserves of glucose and will start converting fat into ketone as an energy source. This is the state you want to be in. The big question is though, how do you know if you are in a state of ketosis?

The easiest way to know is to use a ketogenic stick, which will measure your ketone levels to determine if you are in a state of ketosis. You can buy these from pharmacies or large supermarkets, but if you can't find them there, just check online. You should use them once a week to monitor your progress and make sure you are maintaining your ketone levels. To measure it, you need to take the stick and hold it against your urine. The box you buy will show you the different colors and what they indicate. Usually, dark purple indicates high levels of ketone, whereas very clear indicates low levels. It's best to not drink a lot of water before checking to get the most accurate result. At the same time, being dehydrated will distort the results by concentrating the ketone, so make sure you are adequately hydrated to get the best result. Once you have held the stick to your urine, leave it for a few seconds before checking the color against the chart on the box.

Chapter Summary:

In this chapter, we looked at the main challenges you may face when on the keto diet.

- The main challenges to overcome are in the initial phase. These temporary unpleasant states include feelings of fatigue, muscle weakness, moodiness, low energy levels, and low blood sugar levels.

- It's important to remember that these feelings will pass and it is your body's way of adjusting to a new metabolic state.

- Having a restricted diet can be hard. The ways to overcome this include getting into the habit of counting carbs, stocking your kitchen with just keto-friendly foods, planning meals out in advance, and keeping a handful of keto snacks with you to avoid going off track.

- To check if you are in a state of ketosis, use a ketogenic stick to measure your levels of ketone. It will help you to monitor your progress and make necessary tweaks. It is also motivating to see how your body is changing thanks to your efforts.

In the next chapter, we will look at cheating on the ketogenic diet and answer the big questions – what about cheat days?

Chapter Five: Cheating On The Ketogenic Diet

In this chapter, we will look at cheating on the diet. The occasional slip up happens in all diets and you shouldn't feel bad about it if it does. Let it go and get back on track as soon as possible. However, you should always try to avoid excessive binges or cheat days.

So, let's talk about cheating. Can you have cheat meals on the keto diet?

It is normal among dieters to factor in a once a week 'cheat meal' that allows them some slack and gives them something to look forward to food-wise. However, the keto diet isn't just a diet. It's a lifestyle and one that tends to be stricter than the majority of low-carb diets. What this means is that if you have a cheat meal, it can have a higher impact on your progress than for other diets.

To get a grip on just how cheating on a ketogenic diet can affect you, let's take a look at the disadvantages of cheat meals.

☐   Cheating, even just once, can make you leave a state of ketosis. This is even more true if you eat something that is loaded with carbs. Why is it so easy to leave ketosis? Remember, your body will naturally want to use glucose as an energy source, purely because it's easy to produce. The minute you fill your body with carbs, you flood your system with easy-to-use glucose. It will then take you some time to get back into ketosis because you need to

196

wait for the glucose supplies to leave your body. Measure your ketone levels if you are concerned after eating a specific meal.

☐ To make your body start burning fat for fuel involves a complex metabolic process. The side effects you may feel in the initial stages of going on the keto diet are the result of your body using new hormones and adjusting the production of certain enzymes to help burn fat. By eating cheat meals, it prevents your body from completing this process, and consequently, from staying in ketosis. In the long run, this means you won't be burning fat and you'll have to restart the process all over again.

☐ The keto diet is great for those with diabetes, as it helps control the level of glucose in the blood. Eating a cheat meal loaded with carbs counters this benefit and causes spikes in your blood sugar levels. Not only does this cancel out the positives of the keto diet, it can be dangerous.

☐ Cheating will cause cravings. Just as you're getting used to the healthy, wholesome food on the keto diet, the minute you eat something off the menu, it kickstarts your prior attachment to that food and will make you want more. It may leave you having to readjust to eating low-carb again.

☐ Remember how the keto flu can kick in during the beginning stages of the keto diet? By having cheat meals, your body has to readapt to burning fat instead of glucose, which can bring on those symptoms of the keto flu again. These unpleasant effects include headaches, fatigue, and generally feeling run down.

So, what do you do if you really want to do the keto diet but the idea of not having a cheat meal seems way too restrictive? The good news is that although it is better to follow the keto diet as strictly as possible, there are some alternatives that will cut you a bit of slack.

How To Cheat Sensibly On The Keto Diet

First things first, to get the most out of the ketogenic diet, it's best to follow it as strictly as possible. If you do slip up and eat carbs once in a while, don't be harsh on yourself. In the grand scheme of things, one off-moment will actually make little difference. It's when it becomes regular that it starts to become a concern.

If you want to incorporate a few cheat meals into your ketogenic diet, then here are the best ways to do it. It will slow down the process compared to following the keto diet strictly, but you will still be making progress and reaping the health benefits of the keto diet. There are two main options:

☐   There is a kind of keto diet known as the CKD, or the Cyclical Ketogenic Diet. What this does is follow the keto diet that we have discussed in this book for five days – Monday to Friday, for example. Then, on the weekend, you can eat normally with carbs. This doesn't mean you should pile on the carbs, but it allows certain treats like the odd glass of wine and wholemeal bread. The downside is this will probably take you out of ketosis. The good news is, it still gives some health benefits, preserves muscle mass, and helps make the diet far easier to stick to.

☐ The other option is to stick to your keto diet and instead of making the cheat meal loaded in carbs, make the cheat meal one that is relatively keto-friendly and that you will really enjoy. Don't cheat because you are driven to binge for emotional reasons. Try to identify why you want to cheat on the diet and try to find a healthy substitute for what you are craving. For example, if you want pizza, make one with almond flour, which is far better on the keto diet. This will help to avoid binging and craving more non-friendly keto food after.

It can't be said enough, though – the best form of the keto diet is when you follow it properly. This will bring you the highest number of health benefits and you will feel great for it.

So, what happens if you've been following it correctly and then suddenly, you have one slip up?

Getting Back Into Ketosis After Cheating

☐ Firstly, be kind to yourself. Sometimes, cheating is not exactly 'cheating'. Eating an entire doughy pizza is, unfortunately, cheating, but eating something that is not exactly perfect for keto is fine now and again. Keto is a lifestyle, not something to make you feel guilty or miserable. Try doing the best you can and if you eat the occasional pack of popcorn at the cinema or biscuit with your coffee, let it go and keep focus on your keto diet for the rest of the day.

☐ Don't rationalize your cheat meal with the idea that now that you have cheated, you may as well just carry on for the rest of the day. Instead, after a cheat, make that your

199

last one, as this will reduce the time it takes to get back in ketosis. A one-day binge can take a few days to get back into ketosis. A one-off cheat will be much easier and quicker to get back on track and you may find that you are actually still in a state of ketosis.

☐ After a cheat, make sure your next foods are high in fat and very low in carbs and low in proteins. This will help balance the effect and make getting back into ketosis a bit easier.

☐ If you have eaten a high-carb snack or meal, try doing some exercise afterwards. A walk is fine, but the best thing to do is to do an intensive weight lifting or high intensity workout session. This will help use up that glucose in your system and force your body to use the glycogen stored up in the muscles. By doing this, you will return to ketosis much quicker or even manage to stay in ketosis.

☐ Plan as much as possible and figure out when and why you cheat. This will help you know what to do in these situations. For example, do you find yourself snacking on junk food when you are out? In that case, try taking keto-snacks with you wherever you go. Maybe you get cravings at certain times of the month, especially for women on hormonal cycles. Figure out what it is you are craving and prepare a similar yet keto-friendly substitute for these kinds of moments.

☐ After a cheat meal, drink lots and lots of water. This will help you feel full and help you only eat again when you are actually genuinely hungry.

☐ Just because one day you had lots of extra calories, it doesn't mean you should eat fewer calories the next day.

The idea is to keep eating nutritious food to ward off cravings and remain healthy.

☐ Don't worry if you get out of ketosis. Try to avoid this happening, of course, but keep your morale high – you will be back in it again soon. Most of all, don't beat yourself up over it. The worst thing you can do is demotivate yourself by making yourself feeling guilty. Draw a line under it and move on.

☐ Try to remember why you started the keto diet in the first place. Use that to reconsider your relationship with food. Your body doesn't need loads of carbs to survive and thinking of food as eating to live the best life you can give your body rather than living to eat can really help you get a perspective the next time you fancy something carb-filled or sugary.

Chapter Summary:

In this chapter, we have looked at cheating on the keto diet.

- The best possible thing you can do in regard to cheating is to not do it! But if it happens, don't worry too much. Carry on with keto-friendly foods.

- There are several disadvantages to cheating on the keto diet. The main one is that it can have a dramatic impact on your diet. It can also take you out of ketosis.

- There are ways of incorporating cheating into your diet – such as the Cyclical Ketogenic Diet or simply stocking up on keto-friendly cheats – but be aware that it will affect the results and progress of the keto diet.

- If you do cheat, there are some simple points to follow afterward. Firstly, and most importantly, be kind to yourself. Everyone slips up now and again. Drink lots of water, don't extend the cheat eating for long, and eat high-fat foods after.

In the next chapter, we will look at the best ways of incorporating the keto diet into your lifestyle, especially if you have specific needs.

Chapter Six: Incorporating The Keto Diet Into Your Lifestyle, Whatever Your Needs

In this chapter, we will look at how you can make the ketogenic diet fit into your lifestyle no matter your needs. This chapter will show you how to modify meals to be suitable for your specific requirements, what to eat under particular circumstances, and how to adapt the keto diet if you exercise heavily.

The keto diet can be adapted and tweaked to fit your particular needs. We will look how you can slot a keto diet into your life if you work out, if you include intermittent fasting, if you have allergies, and if you are very busy or have a family who are not on the keto diet. The last one can be particularly challenging, as when everyone around you is eating what was your regular food, it can be a huge test of your willpower. We'll address each of these issues over the course of this chapter.

Keto Dieting And Working Out

One of the big questions for those who regularly exercise and want to try the keto diet is – can I still exercise when on the keto diet? Carbohydrates are the primary source of energy for the body, so a diet where this macronutrient is drastically reduced leaves people wondering how they can exercise in a state of ketosis. However, there are ways to exercise on a keto diet and we will look at this here.

First of all, it is important to know that eating fresh, natural food is vital to fuel the body correctly. The old-saying of 'you are what you eat' couldn't be any more true, so always try eating quality food on the keto diet. The emphasis on eating higher fat content doesn't have anything to do with being able to eat double the number of fast food meals. Your energy should be coming from oils, nuts, meats, dairy products, seafood, and vegetables. To be able to exercise to the best of your ability, this is the first step you should take.

Next, you need to see under which category of exercise your regular workout routine falls under. There are four major exercise categories. Why are these so important? Your body reacts differently when it is subjected to different types of exercise, principally the type of fuel it uses. This is important, as it will be a major factor when deciding what you should and shouldn't eat.

Here are the four different categories of exercise:

- **Aerobic exercise.** This is your cardio group and includes running, aerobic classes, cycling, and swimming. It is considered low intensity, as your heart beat increases and remains at that level without your getting overly out of breath. Cardio burns fat and is a great form of exercise for those doing the keto diet.

- **Anaerobic exercise.** This is high intensity and causes your heart rate to accelerate quickly until you feel you have reached your threshold. It is any kind of exercise that has short exertions of intense energy, such as sprinting in intervals, the popular HIIT sessions (high intensity interval training), and weight training. When you are doing any kind of anaerobic exercise, it will burn carbohydrates. This means just fat will not be enough and will not give you all the energy that you need.

☐ **Stability exercises.** This is low intensity exercise that helps improve the stability of your body by aligning your body, controlling its movement, and strengthening your muscles. It includes core training and exercises to improve your balance.

☐ **Flexibility exercises.** Yoga is a prime example of flexibility exercise. It is a low intensity kind of exercise and is great for working to better your joints, increase the range of motion in your muscles, increase your flexibility, and stretch out your muscles.

So, why does all this matter? While the low intensity workouts – such as any exercise that falls under the stability exercises, the flexibility exercises, and the aerobic exercises – burn fat, so a keto diet is perfectly complementary with these kinds of workout routines. This means you can follow the standard keto diet, exercise as normal, and still remain healthy.

However, anaerobic exercises depend on carbohydrates and will use them to burn fuel. When working under high intensity, your body will not burn fat as effectively. Does that mean that if you weight lift you shouldn't do the keto diet? Not at all. It may be a struggle in the beginning, as your body gets used to switching from burning glucose regularly to burning fat, but there is a way to be on the keto diet and weight lifting.

Targeted Ketogenic Dieting

If you do high intensity exercise, then you will have to adjust your diet to give you the fuel that you need. High intensity will include working out three or more times per week weight lifting, taking spinning classes, or sprinting. You will need a higher portion of carbs, otherwise your performance will be seriously reduced.

To remain in a state of ketosis while doing high intensity exercises, you need to do something called targeted ketogenic dieting and it is really easy. 30 minutes before and after you exercise, eat about 30 grams of fast-acting carbohydrates – fruit or white bread with honey, for example. By doing this in this concentrated window of time, it gives your muscles enough glycogen to perform effectively and feeds your body the carbohydrates it needs during the high intensity exercise and afterwards to recover. Eating carbs this way on a keto diet will prevent you from leaving your state of ketosis.

In time, your body will get used to this and become highly effective at burning fat, providing you with steady energy levels as your blood sugar levels remain controlled and consistent.

When it comes to muscle building, there are some common myths surrounding it. Let's take a look at some of them and see how you can still build significant muscle gains on a low carb diet.

One common misconception is that you need carbohydrates to build muscle. However, the main macronutrient you need is protein, which is considered the building blocks of muscle. In fact, you should be eating about 1 gram of protein for every pound of lean body mass you have – that is the mass of your muscles, excluding the fat. Another essential part of growing muscle is to eat a calorie surplus where you actually eat more calories than you burn. This will help you grow mass. Another important part that is often surprisingly overlooked is that you must train correctly. Many people think lifting as weights heavy as they can manage is the most important thing, but often when people lift too heavy, they let their technique slip, which means the muscle isn't being properly used.

If these are the three most important things, why are carbs considered so important? Because they are important to provide glycogen to the muscles. With targeted ketogenic dieting, you can still get enough carbs without leaving a ketosis state. It is true that with carbs you gain mass quicker – although this mass is mostly fat and not muscle. Carbs by themselves do not produce muscle, they create fuel. It is also worth noting that protein also creates glycogen which will help you get the energy you need for high intensity workouts.

So, while you will need the extra carbs before and after your training, the rest of the nutrients you need to gain muscle and give you energy to perform will be provided by the food in the keto diet. It is unlikely that you will lose muscle mass on the keto diet, as you will be eating a moderate amount of protein anyway.

You may notice that your mass gain is slower on the keto diet, but that is because you are gaining lean mass rather than gaining fat from carbs.

Some people are concerned that the keto diet may affect performance, but the truth is that your body will adapt to the ketosis and that it can perform just as well burning fat as it can burning glucose. It is worth noting that your body will suffer a bit in the beginning as it switches from one metabolic process to the other. This is normal, as this process involves a huge hormonal shift and a period of adaptation. Within a couple of weeks, your body will start converting fat naturally and you will notice that your performance improves and that fat can be a great source of energy for endurance exercises as well as strength exercises.

Studies that compare a high-carb diet and a low-carb diet on long endurance athletes have found little difference between results, showing that low-carb diets can still contribute just as well to performance. One specific study showed that the low-carb athletes burnt just fat, taking huge amounts of energy from fat during a three-hour race. They also didn't show any higher levels of fatigue than the high-carb runners. Not only that, but the low-carb runners didn't show any signs of muscle tissue being broken down, so their bodies were truly fat-burning machines.

As we have already mentioned, a low-carb diet supports low intensity workouts, as they both burn fat. The only time when a standard keto diet is not as effective performance-wise is for high-intensity workouts. However, eating 30 grams of carbs before and after your workout can fix that issue and increase the effectiveness of the keto diet for strength training, too.

Here are some advantages to training on a low-carb and a high-fat diet:

- ☐ Fat is actually essential to supporting testosterone levels, whereas carbs will actually cause a reduction in testosterone. When your testosterone levels drop, it means your body actually holds onto more fat.

- ☐ You will have a much higher level of energy from fat than you will from glycogen. On average, a person can store about 500 grams of glycogen in their body at any one time. Fat, on the other hand, is much easier to store and can technically be stored in huge amounts. This means that you have a much bigger energy reserve from fat.

- ☐ A low-carb diet reduces water retention, which helps you feel lighter and more comfortable when you are training, as well as helping you to look leaner.

So, that is how you can do a keto diet and exercise. The adjustment is easy to make. Now, let's look at how you can do the keto diet while also including intermittent fasting.

Intermittent Fasting

The first question here is, what is intermittent fasting?

Intermittent fasting is basically where you eat only between a certain period per day. During this period, you eat all the calories you need for that day and the rest of the time you will be fasting. For example, perhaps your eating period is between 11am and 5pm. During those six hours, you will eat your day's calories. The other 18 hours of the day, you don't eat anything (some of those hours will be when you are sleeping).

There are actually three types of intermittent fasting. These are:

☐ When you skip meals, usually breakfast.

☐ Eating only during a set period like we saw above. This is the most popular and easiest to maintain.

☐ One to two day fasting where you don't eat for over 24 hours.

If you are going to try intermittent fasting, it is recommended to try the window-eating type first and see how that works for you before attempting longer periods.

The eating period is typically between four and seven hours. So, why do people do this? This practice of fasting for long periods of time and eating for short periods of time is meant to be good for weight loss, digestion, and other health benefits.

Our focus here is keto dieting, so we won't go into depth about intermittent fasting. However, in a nutshell, it is long periods of

209

fasting and small windows of eating. Some people like to combine intermittent fasting and keto dieting as they tend to complement each other. Fasting is one way of getting the glucose stores out of your body and can actually help make the process of starting keto dieting a bit easier, especially by avoiding the 'keto flu,' which you can get during the switchover from using glucose to using fat as fuel.

If you decide you want to do both intermittent fasting and keto dieting, then there are some things you can do to help ease the process.

☐ You need to make sure that you eat enough calories for what you need. Not only that, but the food you eat should be nutritious, healthy, and not processed. Fasting means that you tend to eat fewer calories per day anyway, as it can be harder to fit everything in during that short window and you naturally have a lower appetite. Given this, it is important to make sure you are getting all the nutrients you need while still eating low-carb. If you think you aren't getting enough vitamins, you can check this with a doctor and take multivitamin supplements to get everything you need.

☐ During the eating period, you need to make sure you are eating plenty of fat and not overdoing it on the protein, as this can actually be converted into glucose. To know your ketone levels, use a ketone stick to tell you whether or not you are still in ketosis. This will help you monitor what you are eating and guide you to where you may need to make tweaks to your diet.

Ketogenic Diet With Allergies

If you have allergies, the keto diet may or may not be tricky for you, depending on your allergies.

I will explain. The keto diet is low-carb, so if you have a gluten sensitivity, then it can be a great diet. Foods that typically contain copious amounts of gluten can be replaced with ingredients such as coconut or almond flour to create delicious meals and snacks. You can eliminate gluten entirely from your diet and still have plenty of food choices available to you.

Likewise, if you are dairy intolerant or allergic, then there are plenty of substitutes, such as coconut cream instead of milk or cream and ghee instead of butter. So, eliminating dairy from your diet is relatively easy, too.

The issue is if you have several of a few different allergies. The keto diet is high in fat, which comes from foods such as seafood, eggs, tree nuts, soy, shellfish, and peanuts. If you have allergies to a few of these items, it may restrict your diet a lot more. That doesn't mean you can't do the keto diet – you just have to be extra careful about what you can eat and plan your meals in advance.

The good thing is there are still substitutes. For example, you can cut out seafood and shellfish by replacing it with chicken, pork, or beef. Nuts can be replaced by roasted zucchini or kale for snacks. Eggs are harder to replace on the keto diet, but it's not entirely impossible. The main concern is to make sure you are still getting all the vitamins you need, so you may need to take a multivitamin supplement to guarantee this.

How To Follow The Keto Diet If You Are Very Busy Or Have A Non-Keto Family

Let's first address the issue of not finding time to follow the keto diet. There are really only two solutions to this. The first is to cut back on your current schedule and reduce your busy time and increase your free time. You are probably thinking, if only it were that simple! So that leaves us with option two: preparation. The key to the keto diet, or any kind of diet for that matter, is preparation. If you plan your meals in advance, then you won't be tempted to slip into that dangerous spiral of ordering a quick take-away or eating a carb-loaded snack as a one-off. The problem is, it rarely is a one-off, and repeated 'one-offs' will take you out of ketosis. If you make a week's worth of meals in advance and have plenty of keto snacks available, the chances of not sticking to the diet are much less likely. If you can spare a couple of hours on a Sunday, you can quickly whip up several meals for the days ahead and this will help you stay on track. Remember to take keto-snacks out with you so that you always have a healthy bite to eat when you are feeling peckish.

The next issue is trying to follow the keto diet when your family doesn't. This can be tricky. While you are following a low-carb diet, it can take incredible willpower to resist eating off-the-keto-menu items when others around you are eating (and enjoying!) them. The ideal situation would be to draw the whole family into a keto diet, too. It may not work, but it's worth a try.

If they don't agree, then there are a couple of things you can do:

☐ Clear out one cupboard and have this cupboard all to yourself. This will contain only keto foods and will help you keep your focus. If you continue to mix your food, it will be harder to stick to your goals when there is bread, cakes, and whatever else in your eyeline. Keep the foods separate and out of sight. Out of sight, out of mind can really work wonders in these situations.

☐   You can ask your family for help. Sometimes it is hard to begin the keto diet and then still make your kids' sandwiches, especially in the beginning stage. The temptation will be high. In the first couple of weeks, explain to your family what you are doing and ask them to help out by making their own meals for a while. This will allow you to adapt and build your willpower. Before long, keto eating will become a lifestyle, but it may take a bit of time to get there. This is why a little bit of help can really go a long way.

☐   Planning ahead will help you enormously. It means your meals are all ready to eat and that you have something instantly ready to eat that is good for your keto diet whenever you feel tempted to eat something high in carbs.

☐   Have a flexible eating schedule. Having days where you eat your keto dinner and your family eat their meal is fine. However, you can ask for days where everyone eats a keto meal. That means your willpower isn't tested every day and you don't feel isolated doing the diet alone.

Chapter Summary:

In this chapter, we looked at how you can adjust your diet to cater for your individual needs.

- We covered four main areas where adjustments may be more drastic or necessary.

- The first was how to tweak your keto diet to provide enough energy for optimal performance when you train. If you do low intensity exercise, you can follow a standard keto diet and it won't affect the level of your performance. If you do high intensity exercise – such as sprinting or weight training – you should eat an extra 30 grams of carbohydrates before and after your workout to give you the extra energy and glucose your muscles need.

- Next, we looked at intermittent fasting where you eat during a period of six hours per day and then fast the rest of the day. You can do this with the keto diet and it is popular to combine the two. You just need to make sure that you are getting enough calories and nutrients in this period and that you don't overeat protein, as this will affect your levels of ketone.

- Then we looked at how you can deal with allergies on the keto diet. If you have a gluten or dairy allergy, it is pretty easy to completely eliminate them from your diet and replace them with keto alternatives. The keto diet naturally contains several typical foods that are associated with allergies, though, such as nuts, shellfish, and eggs, so you may need to plan a bit more if you have these types of allergies.

- Finally, we saw what you can do if you are busy or have a family that doesn't follow a keto diet. The key here is to plan ahead and to ask your family for support.

In the next chapter, we will look at the biggest mistakes made on the keto diet – and how you can avoid them.

Chapter Seven: The Biggest Mistakes On The Keto Diet And How To Avoid Them

In this chapter, we will look at some of the biggest mistake that people make on the keto diet.

If you identify with any of the mistakes below, fear not. These are the most common mistakes among people who do the keto diet and they often occur in the first stages. It has already been mentioned, but it is so important that it can be said again – the keto diet isn't just a diet, but a lifestyle and it can be tricky to adopt it initially. It gets easier, but you're bound to face a few hurdles in the beginning. Being aware of them is the first step.

Not Being Patient

This is common in the first stages. You have been eating carbs your whole life and suddenly you stop. You will feel withdrawal symptoms. It's normal, it's unpleasant, but it's a part of the process of switching from burning carbs for fuel to burning fat instead. You will probably get the keto flu, which isn't nice, but it will eventually pass and then you will be in ketosis and feeling amazing. So be patient and ride it out; don't give up.

Not Eating Enough Fat

Surely it is easy to eat enough fat! As a matter of fact, it's not. Many of us have it ingrained in our minds to avoid fat. It is a hard mindset to get out of. Avoiding carbs has been around for awhile, so it is easy to do, but now you are suddenly eating 75% of your daily calorie intake in fats. Make sure you eat plenty of foods like avocados, butter, oil, eggs, and bacon. It feels strange in the beginning, but it is just a new mindset to get into.

Eating High Levels Of Protein

You need to think of different proteins to eat. Out is the chicken and lean turkey steaks and in is the fatty red meat and bacon. You can still eat chicken, of course, and it is definitely recommended. However, fatty steaks are a much better option. It can be tricky in the beginning to manage your protein levels, so it's good to measure your levels of ketone to make sure you are eating correctly. Too much protein can be converted into glucose, taking you out of your ketosis state.

Eating Hidden Carbs

Don't kick yourself if you end up eating more carbs than you thought you were eating. The thing is, you have to get clued up. Processed foods have all sorts of ways of adding in extra hidden carbs, and in the beginning, you may not know what are carbs and what aren't. It's advisable to read as much as you can about these so you can make better decisions. Be aware of ingredients such as corn syrup, fruit juice, maltose, agave, and dextrose, among many, many more. These are packed with carbs and sugars and should be avoided.

Going It Alone

The keto diet isn't for the faint-hearted and it requires enormous dedication and commitment. It is best to do it with someone who can share your experience, struggles, and achievements. If you don't know anyone who will do the keto diet with you, then join Facebook groups or online forums. Look for local keto groups, which are common, especially in big cities. It means you can meet likeminded people and keep your focus. When you're doing it alone, it can seem overwhelming. When you are part of a larger group, it can make it a whole lot easier.

Not Getting Enough Electrolytes

Electrolytes include sodium, potassium, and magnesium, and if you don't get enough of these, you will feel tired, lethargic, constipated, and suffer from headaches. Keto diets reduce the amount of insulin, which in turn makes the kidneys flush out sodium. You have to replace this to avoid feeling like you have the flu. Eating salty snacks is one way; drinking broth is another. Eating avocados will help bring your potassium levels up and for magnesium, try eating plenty of nuts. Magnesium is a bit harder to get in sufficient quantities, so it may help to take supplements.

Chapter Summary:

In this chapter, we looked at some of the biggest and most common mistakes that are made when starting the keto diet.

- One of the most common mistakes is to give up in the first couple of weeks. You may feel tired and a bit off in the beginning, but this is your body switching to ketosis.

- Another mistake is eating too much protein. Protein only makes up 20% of your calories allowance. 75% should be fats.

- Not eating enough fat can be a problem, as it requires a new mindset. Make sure to carefully monitor in the beginning how much you are eating to make sure you are getting enough of the right foods.

- Eating hidden carbs is all too common, which is why it is recommended to avoid processed foods.

- Doing the keto diet by yourself can be tough. Find a support group to help you share your experiences.

- Finally, make sure you are getting enough electrolytes. These will ward off the feelings of the keto flu.

In the next chapter, we will look at a four-week meal plan to start your keto diet.

Chapter Eight: Four-Week Keto Meal Plan

In this chapter, we will look at a four-week meal plan to help you get started on a keto diet. It is important to remember that everyone has their own set number of calories to eat per day, which you can calculate using the formula in Chapter Two. After doing this, you can adjust the meal plans below to suit your needs.

Note: In this plan, we will measure net carbs. This is fiber subtracted from total carbs to give net carbs. The idea is that the fiber isn't absorbed into the bloodstream, so you only need to concern yourself with net carbs.

Note: The 30 grams of carbs to eat before working out is TOTAL carbs, so make sure you are aware of that difference. The net carbs will vary greatly.

The days in each week make the most of leftovers from previous days to make planning and grocery shopping far easier for you. All the recipes can be found after the tables.

The calories per day is around 1,600 calories, give or take a few calories. To make this simple, the daily amount has been rounded up or rounded down to 1,600 to give clearance for any miscalculations. The grams have all been rounded up or down to the nearest whole number.

These meal plans are a standard keto diet plan and don't take into consideration and allergies or exercise programs you may have. If you do cardio, then you can follow these plans normally. If you weight lift, remember to eat the extra 30 grams of total carbs before and after you work out. Additionally, if you have allergies, seek out alternatives in the ingredients.

Week One

In the first week, you may notice symptoms of the keto flu. To help ease this, drink plenty of water with a pinch of salt. The plan will not include any desserts for the first week.

	Day One	Day Two	Day Three
Breakfast	Scrambled eggs with cheese	Cheese muffins	Scrambled eggs with cheese
Lunch	Bacon burger and spinach salad	Cheesy salad	Chicken and spinach salad
Dinner	Beef stew	Bacon burger	Stir fry with pork
		Spinach salad	
Total Calories/Carbs (net)	1600 / 6.5 grams	1600/7.7 grams	1600/10.5 grams

	Day Four	Day Five	Day Six	Day Seven
Breakfast	Cheese muffins	Scrambled eggs with cheese	Cheese muffins	Scrambled eggs with cheese
Lunch	Spinach salad	Spinach salad with feta cheese	Chicken thighs with spinach salad	Canned tuna with spinach salad.
Dinner	Curried chicken Thighs	Salmon with asparagus	Canned tuna with spinach salad	Keto meatballs
	One avocado with chili flakes and olive oil	Green beans with lemon		Green beans with lemon
Total Calories/Carbs (net)	1600 / 4.5 grams	1600 / 13 grams	1600 / 13 grams	1600 / 9 grams

Image credit: MK Photgrap55

Week Two

This week, you may still be feeling the effects of the keto flu. Don't worry, it will pass. Just keep drinking plenty (and I mean plenty!) of water with added pinches of salt. Don't worry about increased sodium levels from drinking salty water. Your kidneys are currently flushing out sodium from your body, so you need to replace this. This week, we will also begin breakfast with keto coffee, which is high in fats and very low in carbs.

	Day One	Day Two	Day Three
Breakfast	Keto coffee	Keto coffee	Keto coffee
Lunch	Mushroom omelette	Canned tuna and spinach salad	Chicken thighs and spinach salad
Dinner	Salmon with asparagus	Keto meatballs	Mushroom omelette
		Green beans with roasted nuts	Green beans with lemon

Total Calories/Carbs (net)	1600 / 17 grams	1600 / 10 grams	1600 / 12 grams

	Day Four	Day Five	Day Six	Day Seven
Breakfast	Keto coffee	Keto coffee	Keto coffee	Keto coffee
Lunch	Omelette with cheese and ham	Omelette with mushrooms	Meatballs Creamy spinach salad	Burger and creamy spinach salad
Dinner	Burger with creamy spinach and almonds	Curried chicken thighs	Stir fry with pork	Meatballs
		Spinach salad		Green beans with roasted nuts
Total Calories/Carbs (net)	1600 / 10 grams	1600 / 11 grams	1600 / 12 grams	1600 / 10 grams

Image credit: Ovidiu Marian

223

Week Three

This week, we will change it up a bit. Lunch will be nothing more than a light salad. This is a gentle way of introducing fasting, a common part of keto. The morning will be loaded with fats that will keep you ticking until later in the day. Lunch will be a simple salad, which is mostly to keep you in the mindset of eating something. The best part is, dinner will include a full meal and a dessert! The desserts are keto-friendly and will help you stay on track with your goals. If you follow this plan, you will remain in a ketosis state, even with a daily treat!

	Day One	Day Two	Day Three
Breakfast	Keto coffee	Keto coffee	Keto coffee
Lunch	Green salad	Green salad	Green salad
Dinner	Fish coconut curry	Quesadillas	Bacon burger
	Chocolate mousse	Chocolate mousse	Banana waffles
Total Calories/Carbs (net)	1600 / 13 grams.	1600 / 5 grams	1600/ 7 grams

	Day Four	Day Five	Day Six	Day Seven
Breakfast	Keto coffee	Keto coffee	Keto coffee	Keto coffee
Lunch	Green salad	Green salad	Green salad	Green salad
Dinner	Chicken garam masala	Fish coconut curry	Baked Italian meatballs	Chicken garam masala
	Banana waffles	Chocolate mousse	Banana waffles	Chocolate mousse
Total Calories/Carbs (net)	1600 / 10 grams	1600 / 12 grams	1600 / 13 grams	1600 / 9 grams

Image credit: Keystone Pixels

Week Four

After a week of an introduction to fasting, we are now going back to a regular three meals per day. However, those experienced with keto dieting often use the fourth week to do full-on intermittent fasting, where they skip breakfast and lunch and use the final hours of the day to eat. Alternatively, they may fast in the morning and eat from midday until 6 pm. If you are new to keto, this could be a bit extreme, which is why we are going back to a regular meal plan. However, it could be something you may like to consider in the future. In week four, we will stick to keto coffee, as it's possibly one of the best ways to start the day.

	Day One	Day Two	Day Three
Breakfast	Keto coffee	Keto coffee	Keto coffee
Lunch	Avocado with eggs and smoked salmon	Fish coconut curry	Avocado with eggs and ham
Dinner	Pork stir fry	Mushroom and cheese omelette	Pork stir fry

			Creamy spinach
Total Calories/Carbs (net)	1600 / 7 grams	1600 / 9 grams	1600 / 8 grams
	Day Four	Day Five	Day Six	Day Seven
Breakfast	Keto coffee	Keto coffee	Keto coffee	Keto coffee
Lunch	Quesadillas	Mushroom and cheese omelette	Meatballs	Quesadillas
Dinner	Ham and cheese omelette	Meatballs	Avocado with eggs and smoked salmon	Pork stir fry
	Creamy spinach salad		Green beans with roasted nuts	Avocado salad
Total Calories/Carbs (net)	1600 / 6 grams	1600 / 9 grams	1600 / 7 grams	1600 / 14 grams

Image credit: 5PH

Cheesy Muffins

This recipe serves 4 people.

A serving contains 2 grams of carbohydrates.

Ingredients:

- 6 eggs.
- 2 spring onions.
- A handful of spinach leaves.
- 140 grams of cooked bacon.
- 85 grams of shredded cheese (cheddar or parmesan works well).
- Salt and pepper, to taste.

Method:

1 – Chop the spring onions and the bacon. While doing that, fry the spinach leaves quickly in a frying pan with a sprinkle of olive oil until they wilt.

2 – Mix the eggs in the bowl with the cheese and the seasoning. Add the spring onions, the bacon, and the spinach leaves.

3 – Pour the mixture into a muffin tray.

4 – Bake for about 15 minutes (it may take a bit long if your muffin tray is big).

Image credit: EQRoy

Scrambled Eggs With Cheese

This recipe serves 4 people.

A serving contains 2 grams of carbohydrates.

Ingredients:

- 6 eggs.
- A dollop of cream cheese.
- 100 grams of shredded cheddar or parmesan cheese.
- 2 tablespoons of full-fat butter.
- Salt and pepper to taste.

Method:

1 – Whisk the eggs and put in the pan. Scramble together with the salt and the pepper, three quarters of the grated cheese, and the all of the cream cheese.

2 – Serve on a plate and the add the rest of the grated cheese. Top with a sprinkle of parsley (optional).

Image credit: marcin jucha

Bacon Burger

This recipe serves 1 person.

A serving has 1 gram of carbs.

Ingredients:

- 200 grams of minced beef.
- 2 slices of chopped bacon.
- A small handful of cheddar cheese (grated).
- 1 tablespoon of crushed garlic.
- 1 tablespoon of soy sauce.
- Half a tablespoon of onion powder.
- A sprinkle of chopped chives.
- A dash of Worcestershire sauce.
- Salt and pepper, to taste.

Method:

1 – Cook the bacon in a frying pan. Take two-thirds of the cooked bacon and mix in a separate bowl with the beef and the spices (both liquid and dry).

2 – Form a couple of patties using the mix.

3 – Cook the patties in the same pan as you cooked the bacon to get all that lovely fat.

4 – Once cooked well on both sides, serve with the extra bacon and a few slices of cheese.

5 – Serve with a salad made with spinach, chopped avocado, rocket, lettuce, and a drizzle of olive oil and chili flakes.

Image credit: Dragunov

Beef Stew

Ingredients:

- 225 grams of chunky beef.
- 250 grams of beef broth.
- Coconut oil.
- ¼ of an onion.
- Zest and juice of half an orange.
- A splash of soy sauce.
- A splash of fish sauce.
- 1 tablespoon of thyme.
- 1 clove of crushed garlic.
- ½ tablespoon of sage.
- ½ tablespoon of rosemary.
- 1 bay leaf.

Method:

1 – Add coconut oil to a pan on high heat. Throw in the chunks of beef with the zest of the orange and a seasoning of salt and pepper. Sear the meat.

2 – Take the meat out of the pan once it is a nice brown and then add in the vegetables until slightly soft.

3 – Add the orange juice and the rest of the ingredients except the sage, rosemary, and thyme.

4 – Let it cook for a couple of minutes and then transfer the mixture into a large crock pot. Let it cook for about 3 hours.

5 – Then add in the sage, rosemary, and thyme. Leave for another hour or so on a low heat.

Image credit: gkrphoto

Chicken And Spinach Salad

This recipe serves 2 people.

A serving contains 4 grams of carbohydrates.

Ingredients:

- 500 grams of chicken breast.
- 1 avocado.
- 2 tablespoons of full-fat butter.
- A handful of mixed nuts.
- A handful of spinach leaves.
- 50 grams of feta cheese crumbled up.
- Salt and pepper, to taste.
- A sprinkle of olive oil (to dress the rocket and avocado).

Method:

1 – Add the chicken breasts to a pan and cook in the butter on low heat. Cook each side until golden brown. Prick the chicken to test that it's cooked – if clear liquid runs out, it's cooked.

2 – Put the spinach leaves on a plate with the feta cheese and mixed nuts sprinkled over. Sprinkle with olive oil, salt, and a bit of pepper before serving the chicken on top. Add some sliced avocado, too (optional).

Image credit: Elenadesign

Stir Fry With Pork

This recipe serves 2 people.

Each serving contains 5 grams of carbohydrates.

Ingredients:

- 340 grams of pork shoulder slices.
- 2 green peppers sliced.
- 2 spring onions sliced.
- 110 grams of butter.
- 2 tablespoons almonds.
- 1 teaspoon of chili paste.
- Salt and pepper, to taste.

Method:

1 –Put the butter in a frying pan (or a wok if you have one) and fry the pork, the peppers, and the spring onions. Save a bit of this butter for serving.

2 – Cook until the meat is brown. Add the vegetables and the chili paste and then season with salt and pepper.

3 – When it's all cooked, transfer onto a plate and serve with a dollop of butter and a sprinkle of almonds.

Image credit: AKIRACOKI

Curried Chicken Thighs

Ingredients:

- 2 chicken thighs.
- Olive oil.
- Salt and pepper.
- ½ tablespoon of yellow curry powder.
- ½ tablespoon of cumin.
- ½ tablespoon of paprika.
- ½ tablespoon of garlic powder.
- ¼ tablespoon of cayenne pepper.
- ¼ tablespoon of allspice.
- ¼ tablespoon of chili powder.
- ¼ tablespoon of coriander.
- A pinch of cinnamon, ginger powder, salt, and pepper.

Method:

1 – Mix all the spices in a bowl and rub into the chicken thighs.

2 – Bake for about 40 minutes until the skin gets crispy.

3 – Leave to cool and serve with a big green salad.

Image credit: Martin Dopirak

Salmon With Asparagus

This recipe serves 2 people.

Each serving has 2 grams of carbohydrates.

Ingredients:

- 225 grams of green asparagus.
- 85 grams of butter.
- 340 grams of salmon. Organic is the best.
- Salt and pepper, to taste.

Method:

1 – Add a large chunk of butter to the frying pan and fry the asparagus over a medium heat for about 4 minutes. Add in a bit more butter and then add the salmon.

2 – Cook the salmon on both sides for a couple of minutes.

3 – Once everything is cooked, season the salmon and serve on a plate with the rest of the butter.

Image credit: Jacek Chabraszewsk

Keto Meatballs

This recipe serves 4 people.

A serving contains 1 gram of carbohydrates.

Ingredients:

- 680 grams of ground beef.
- 2 tablespoons of full-fat butter.
- 150 grams of grated cheese (cheddar or parmesan is great).
- 100 grams of mayonnaise.
- 4 tablespoons of pickled jalapenos.
- 1 tablespoon of chili powder (or paprika if you prefer).
- 1 tablespoon of Dijon mustard.
- Salt, pepper, and cayenne pepper, to taste.

Method:

1 – Mix the mayonnaise, the jalapenos, the chili powder, the Dijon mustard, the cayenne pepper, 100 grams of the cheddar cheese, and a hint of salt and pepper.

2 – Once well mixed, add the ground beef.

3 – Mix together and create meatballs from the mix.

4 – Fry them in butter until cooked all the way through. Serve with the extra cheddar cheese sprinkled over the top.

Image credit: sebasnoo

Green Beans With Lemon

A serving contains 3 grams of carbs.

Ingredients:

- 225 grams of green beans.
- Olive oil.
- Half a lemon – its juice and its zest.
- A sprinkle of parmesan cheese.
- Crushed garlic.
- Salt, to taste.

Method:

1 – Spread the green beans out on a baking tray. Add the olive oil, the lemon zest and juice, the garlic, and the salt. Bake for about 20 minutes.

2 – When cooked, put on a plate and serve with a sprinkle of cheese.

Image credit: Brent Hofacker

Keto Coffee

This has 1 gram of carbs, but 30 grams of fat.

Ingredients:

- 1 cup of hot coffee. Brew it just before you make this to keep the coffee fresh.
- 1 tablespoon of coconut oil.
- 1 tablespoon of full-fat butter (use unsalted).
- 1 tablespoon of thick cream.

Method:

1 – Mix all the ingredients together until smooth. Drink while hot. If you like your coffee extra sweet, add some drops of stevia liquid sweetener.

Image credit: SewCream

Mushroom Omelette

This recipe serves 1 person.

Each serving has 4 grams of carbohydrates.

Ingredients:

- 3 eggs (organic, free-range for the best taste and healthiest option).
- 30 grams of butter.
- 30 grams of grated cheese (parmesan is a good choice, but any other kind of hard cheese will work).
- ¼ of an onion.
- 3 big mushrooms chopped up.
- Salt and pepper, to taste.

Method:

1 – Break the eggs into a bowl. Add some salt and pepper and whisk until totally smooth.

2 – Melt butter in a frying pan and then pour in the egg mixture.

3 – When the bottom of the egg is firm but the top is a little bit runny, sprinkle on the cheese, the onion, and the mushroom.

4 – Leave it to cook a little longer then fold it in half. It will be ready when it is golden brown.

Image credit: Wong yu Liang

Creamy Spinach

Ingredients:

- A big handful of spinach leaves.
- 25 grams of butter.
- 25 grams of cheddar cheese.
- Salt, to taste.
- A sprinkle of chili leaves.

Method:

1 – Add the butter to a frying pan and melt. Add the cheese to get a melted, buttery sauce.

2 – Mix in the spinach leaves and take everything out once the spinach leaves begin to wilt.

3 – Sprinkle with salt and chili leaves.

Image credit: Brent Hofacker

Fish Coconut Curry

This recipe serves 2 people.

Each serving contains 5 grams of carbohydrates.

Ingredients:

- 700 grams of chunky white fish (cod is great, but anything similar works, too).
- 30 grams of butter.
- Salt and pepper.
- 4 tablespoons of ghee.
- 2 tablespoons of red curry paste (or green, if you prefer).
- 400 grams of coconut cream (unsweetened).
- 8 tablespoons of cilantro or parsley, chopped.
- 450 grams of cauliflower.

Method:

1 – Put the fish pieces in the baking tray. Season with salt and pepper and add butter on the top.

2 – Mix the coconut cream, the chopped cilantro or parsley, and the curry paste. Pour all over the fish.

3 – Bake for about 20 minutes. In the meantime, parboil the cauliflower and blend into rice-sized bits for a low-carb version of rice.

Image credit: Sta

Quesadillas

This recipe serves 3 people.

Each serving contains 5 grams of carbohydrates.

Ingredients:

For the tortillas:

- 2 eggs.
- 2 egg whites.
- 170 grams of cream cheese.
- 1 ½ tablespoons of ground psyllium husk powder (or flaxseed meal).
- 1 tablespoon of coconut flour (or almond flour).
- Salt, to taste.

For the filling:

- 140 grams of grated cheese (cheddar or any kind of hard cheese).
- A bunch of leafy greens, such as spinach, rocket, and lettuce.
- 1 tablespoon of olive oil.

Method:

1 – Mix the eggs and the egg whites together. Add the cream cheese and mix until the mixture is perfectly smooth. You can do this with a fork or just pop it all into a mixer.

2 – In a different bowl, mix the salt, the coconut flour, and the psyllium husk powder. Gradually add this dry mixture into the eggy mixture from the first step. Keep mixing the eggy mixture as you're doing it. Let it set a little while and mix again. It will eventually get the consistency of pancake batter.

3 – Create six tortilla circles on a baking tray and cook for about 5 minutes. Keep an eye on them. Once they look golden brown, they're done.

4 – Now that you have the tortillas, it is time to make your quesadillas. Take three tortillas and divide half the grated cheese between them.

5 – Add the leafy greens on top of the cheese, add the rest of the cheese, and then add another tortilla on top.

6 – Fry each quesadilla in a frying pan with butter until the cheese melts.

Image credit: Sapunova Svetlana

Chicken Garam Masala

This recipe serves 4 people.

Each serving contains 5 grams of carbohydrates.

Ingredients:

For the chicken:

- 700 grams of organic chicken breast.
- 3 tablespoons of butter.
- Salt, to taste.
- 1 red pepper, chopped.
- 425 grams of full-fat cream.
- Some fresh parsley, chopped.

For the garam masala:

*You can buy this in the supermarket, but it is better to make it from scratch. Not only is it delicious, but you know exactly what is in it and avoid any added sugars.

- 1 teaspoon of ground cumin.
- 2 teaspoons of coriander seeds.
- 1 teaspoon of turmeric.
- 1 teaspoon of ginger.
- 1 teaspoon of cardamom.
- 1 teaspoon of paprika.
- 1 teaspoon of chili powder.
- A hint of ground nutmeg.

Method:

1 – Mix all the spices together.

2 – Cut the chicken breasts into slices and fry slightly.

3 – Add in half of the spices and mix well with the chicken.

4 – Add seasoning, then place the chicken with all its juices into a baking dish.

5 – In a separate bowl, mix the cream, the pepper, and the rest of spices together. Spread this all over the chicken.

6 – Bake for 20 minutes and then serve with a sprinkle of parsley or a few slices of onion.

Image credit: Santhosh Varghese

Avocado Chocolate Mousse

This chocolate mousse is a healthy take on the original, using avocado as its main ingredient. It may sound strange to put avocado and chocolate together, but the result is outstanding, especially for those with a sweet tooth. You can't taste the avocado; rather it gives the mousse a smooth, creamy texture. It's also low in carbs and high in fats, just what you want from a keto dessert.

This recipe serves 1 person.
Each serving contains 6 grams of carbohydrates.

Ingredients:
- ¼ cup of cocoa powder. Use dark cocoa powder that is organic, if possible.
- 1 avocado.
- 10 drops of stevia sweetener.
- ½ tablespoon of vanilla extract.
- A pinch of salt (sounds odd, but it really enhances the flavor).

Method:
1 – Halve the avocado, take the stone out, and scoop the flesh into a bowl.

2 – Add the other ingredients and mix everything together until smooth.

Image credit: Larisa Blinova

Banana Waffles

This recipe makes 8 servings.
A serving contains 7 grams of carbohydrates.

Ingredients:

- 2 big, ripe bananas.
- 4 eggs.
- 250 grams of almond flour.
- 250 grams of coconut milk.
- A pinch of salt.
- 1 teaspoon of baking powder.
- 1 teaspoon of vanilla extract.
- 1 teaspoon of cinnamon.
- 1 tablespoon of ground psyllium husk powder.
- Coconut oil.

Method:

1 – Take all the ingredients and put in a blender. Blend it up and let it settle after.

2 – Spray a waffle maker with some coconut oil and pour in the mixture. Cook until a lovely golden brown.

3 – To serve, use whipped coconut cream or just a dollop of fresh, full-fat butter.

Image credit: Prachana Thong-on

Chapter Summary:

In this chapter, we looked at meal plans for a four-week period.

- The first and second week you may notice some signs of the keto flu. Drink plenty of water to help ease the symptoms.

- The third week has an element of fasting – but also some delicious desserts.

- The fourth week includes three regular meal plans with low carbs and high fat.

Final Words

You have reached the end of *The Clever Ketogenic Meal Plan.* I hope you now feel you have a good foundation of just what the keto diet is all about and feel inspired to continue on this path to a new, healthier lifestyle.

Thank you for reading my book!

The Complete Ketogenic Cookbook

Extensive Selection Of Healthy And Tasty Recipes
To Make Keto Diet Fun And Easy To Follow

Charlotte Melhoff

Introduction

Welcome to *The Complete Ketogenic Cookbook*! First, thank you for downloading this book. Secondly, congratulations for taking the plunge into eating a keto diet! It's not always a smooth journey but you will see that it is more than just a diet – it's a lifestyle. Best of all, there is so much delicious food available for you which is keto-friendly. So, you can eat healthily, lose weight, and eat tasty meals,

Do you want to follow the keto diet but are not sure what you can eat? What if I told you that it isn't as rigid as you may believe and you can still eat amazingly tasty food? Eating well on the keto diet can still include your favourite foods and I'm going to show you how.

I've been following the keto diet for many years now. I wanted to reduce my carbohydrate intake as it made me feel sluggish and bloated so I tried the keto diet. In the beginning, it was hard making this switch but in time, I gradually learnt about the different food I can eat and started experimenting with new, keto-friendly recipes. I missed foods like pizza and curries, yet I began to discover keto-friendly alternatives that I could make easily and it wouldn't affect my dieting progress. Suddenly keto-dieting became easy and it started to become natural for me as I adopted it as a lifestyle. I noticed I shed weight, my skin and hair looked fresh and glossy, and I had bundles of energy.

The key to dieting, I believe, is to not feel like you are missing out and to not go hungry. These two factors make us feel miserable so I created recipes that kept me full for longer and replaced my classic favourites. My meals always work for me so I decided to write this book and share my knowledge and experience with other people who want to follow the keto diet.

I promise that this book will help you cook dozens of delicious recipes that will help you follow a keto diet easily. I hope that the recipes will show you just how easy it is to cut carbs out of our diets and that you will feel inspired to create your own delicious meals as well.

So, stick to your goals and make keto dieting a part of your lifestyle too. Believe me, you won't regret it. Let's move onto the first chapter and begin a new gastronomic journey. We'll start with breakfast - and yes, muffins and waffles are on the menu!

Chapter One: Breakfast Recipes

In this chapter, we will be looking at keto-friendly recipes for breakfast.

The keto diet encourages eating very little carbs and carb intake shouldn't exceed more than 5% of your daily calorie allowance. This small amount of carbs is better off being eaten later in the day and having a breakfast high in fat in the morning. A high-fat breakfast increases your metabolism which in turn helps stimulate fat loss.

Your enzymes are at their most active when you wake up and become gradually less active throughout the day. By the end of the day, your enzymes have slowed right down. Whatever you fuel your body with in the morning will set the pace of your metabolism for the rest of the day. Eating fat will help your body keep in fat-burning mode.

So, what are the best things to eat?

Eggs are a popular choice. Quick and simple to make, they often become a staple ingredient in a keto breakfast. However, you decide to eat them is your choice and the way you cook them doesn't make much difference in terms of effecting your keto diet. Boiling or poaching is one of the purest ways to cook them whereas frying or scrambling them will let you add in extra butter or oil to get an even higher-fat content. Alternatively, you can make an omelette with some low-carb vegetables – mushrooms or spinach are great choices – to add extra flavour and texture. You can even prepare several days' worth of breakfasts by making a quiche without the carbs and plenty of fat with ingredients such as cheese, full-fat cream, and butter.

If you don't want eggs, there are plenty of other choices. For example, mini burgers made from sausage meat and served with cheese and spinach has hardly any carbs but a good quantity of fat, especially if you cook the sausage meat in butter.

Let's look at some low-carb, high fat breakfasts that are great for those on the keto diet. Here are the recipes we will cover in order:

- ☐ Butter-fried egg with chopped avocado and smoked salmon.
- ☐ Bacon and spinach omelette.
- ☐ Mexican scrambled eggs.
- ☐ Avocado breakfast bowls.
- ☐ Egg muffins.
- ☐ Classic bacon and eggs.
- ☐ Keto-style pancakes.
- ☐ Blueberry pancakes.
- ☐ Breakfast bagels.
- ☐ Spinach and cheese wraps.
- ☐ Savoury waffles.
- ☐ Sausage casserole.
- ☐ Lemon and poppy seed muffins.
- ☐ Coconut porridge.
- ☐ Pumpkin spice latte.

Butter-Fried Egg With Chopped Avocado And Smoked Salmon

This delicious breakfast is a great start to the day being high in fat and very low in carbs. It should give you sufficient energy levels as well as keep you full longer, helping you to ward off those mid-morning hunger pangs.

This recipe is for two people.
Each serving has 5 grams of carbohydrates.

Ingredients:

- 4 eggs.
- 140 grams of pure butter.
- 2 avocados.
- A pinch of sea salt and black pepper (to taste).
- 110 grams of smoked salmon.
- A sprinkle of parsley (optional).

Method:

1 – Place the butter in the frying pan on a low heat until it melts. Crack the four eggs into the frying pan, season with salt and pepper, and let them cook in the butter. Cook until the egg white is hard and whether you have the yolk hard or runny is up to you!

2 – Once cooked, take them out and serve on a plate with sliced avocado, a sprinkle of chopped parsley, and some slices of smoked salmon.

Tip: change the flavour by adding chili flakes, fresh dill, or some chopped red onion.

Image credit: Ekaterina Smirnova

Bacon And Spinach Omelette

This recipe is naturally low in carbs, high in fats, and tastes great. It provides an alternative way of eating eggs for breakfast and both the protein and fat content from the eggs will keep hunger away. Although categorised here as a breakfast meal, it can be made in batches and cut into slices as an on-the-go snack, a post-workout bite, or as a light lunch served with a vegetable salad.

This recipe serves one person.
Each serving has 3 grams of carbohydrates.

Ingredients:

- 2 eggs
- 150 grams of bacon chopped into small cubes.
- 85 grams of pure, full-fat butter.
- 55 grams of spinach (fresh or frozen is fine).
- A sprinkle of chives or parsley (optional).
- Sea salt and black pepper to taste.

Method:

1 – Grease a baking dish with some of the butter, enough to cover it in a thin layer of grease.

2 – Put the rest of the butter in a frying pan and fry the bacon and spinach together.

3 – In a bowl, mix the eggs together and then whisk in the fried bacon and spinach. Make sure you pour in all that fat and butter from the frying pan.
4 – Add some of the chopped chives or parsley, if you want. Season with the salt and pepper.

5 – Pour the mixture into the baking dish and bake for about 20 minutes at 200°C. If it has a nice, golden brown look before the 20 minutes are up, then it's probably ready.

6 – Take it out of the baking tray, let it cool down a bit, and then eat.

Tip: Replace the bacon with mushrooms for a change and add a sprinkle of parmesan cheese on top. This is a great alternative for vegetarians.

Image credit: jijieforsythe

Mexican Scrambled Eggs

If you are looking for a way of spicing up eggs in the morning, this Mexican omelette will do just that! Not only does it taste good, but the high fat, low carb content will keep your energy levels high throughout the morning.

This recipe serves 4 people.
A serving contains 2 grams of carbohydrates.

Ingredients:

- 6 eggs.
- 4 spring onions.
- 2 finely chopped jalapenos.
- 1 finely chopped tomato.
- 85 grams of shredded cheddar or parmesan cheese.
- 2 tablespoons of full-fat butter.
- Salt and pepper to taste.

Method:

1 – Chop the spring onions, the jalapenos, and the tomatoes before frying for about 3 minutes in butter.

2 – Whisk the eggs and put in them in the pan. Scramble everything together, serve on a plate and add a topping of the shredded cheese and a hint of salt and pepper.

Tip: serve with some additional chili flakes for added spiciness. You can serve the dish with some sliced avocados for additional fats.

Image credit: sta

Avocado Breakfast Bowls

This recipe is delicious and unusual, making it an excellent choice for when you are looking for something a bit different. It will also keep you full all morning thanks to the high fat content. This is one of the best keto breakfasts to have if you have a long day ahead.

This recipe serves one person.
A serving has 3 grams of carbohydrates.

Ingredients:

- 1 large avocado.
- 2 eggs.
- 2 slices of deli ham.
- 1 tablespoon of olive oil.

Method:

1 – Cut the avocado in half and scoop out the flesh, leaving about half an inch layer inside. Keep the carved out avocado flesh and serve it on the side with a drizzle of olive oil.

2 – Line the inside with a slice of ham per half.

3 – Crack an egg inside each half.

4 – Drizzle with olive oil and pop it inside the oven. Cook for about 10 minutes.

Tip: substitute ham with bacon or with smoked salmon.

Image credit: SewCream

Egg Muffins

Sometimes, a muffin in the morning is all we want. These egg muffins will keep you on your keto-track as well as make you feel satisfied and full.

This recipe serves four people.
A serving contains 2 grams of carbohydrates.

Ingredients:

- 6 eggs.
- 2 spring onions.
- A handful of spinach leaves.
- 140 grams of cooked bacon.
- 85 grams of shredded cheese (cheddar or parmesan works well).
- Salt and pepper to taste.

Method:

1 – Chop the spring onions and the bacon. While doing that, fry the spinach leaves quickly in a frying pan with a sprinkle of olive oil until they wilt.

2 – Mix the eggs in the bowl with the cheese and the seasoning. Add the spring onions, the bacon, and the spinach leaves.

3 – Pour the mixture into a muffin tray.

4 – Bake for about 15 minutes (it may take a bit long if your muffin tray is big).

Tip: Make these in advance to last for a couple of breakfasts or as snacks to be enjoyed whenever hunger strikes. The protein and fat content also make them a great post-workout snack.

Image credit: Elena Shashkina

Classic Bacon And Eggs

This all-time favourite of fried eggs and bacon is a must have in any keto cookbook! Simply, because everyone loves bacon and eggs.

This recipe serves four people.
A serving contains 1 gram of carbohydrates.

Ingredients:

- 8 eggs.
- 150 grams of sliced bacon.
- 2 avocados.

Method:

1 – Fry the bacon until crispy. You can just fry them in their own fat.

2 – Leave the bacon fat in the pan and fry the eggs the way you like them.

3 – Slice the two avocados and distribute them equally among the plates.

4 – Serve the bacon and the eggs.

Tip: Add a few rocket leaves to create a salad and get some additional nutrients in.

Image credit: Ekaterina Markelova

Keto-Style Pancakes

If you are looking for something that is dairy-free, then these pancakes are perfect. They are great for those mornings when you feel like spoiling yourself with something tasty their texture feels just like a regular pancake, giving that pancake satisfaction with very few carbs! To increase the fat content even more, add a dollop of almond butter on top and you can even have them with some chopped raspberries if you fancy something sweet and fresh.

This recipe serves one person.
A serving contains 2 grams of carbohydrates.

Ingredients:

- 20 grams of pork rinds.
- 2 eggs.
- 2 tablespoons of cashew milk, ideally unsweetened.
- 1 teaspoon of maple extract for flavouring.
- 1 teaspoon of cinnamon powder (optional if you don't like cinnamon).
- 2 tablespoons of coconut oil.

Method:

1 – Blend all the pork rinds in a blender until it's in a powdered form. Then, add the rest of the ingredients until it's a smooth paste.

2 – Add one tablespoon of coconut oil in to a frying pan, heat it up on a medium heat and then add a quarter cup of batter into the frying pan.

3 – Cook until firm, give it a flip and cook until the other side is firm too. It takes about 2 minutes one side, one minute the other.

4 – Take out of the frying pan and cook the rest of the batter in the same way, adding more coconut oil if necessary.

Tip: these also make a great snack and are perfect for when you have a hard to control sweet urge, especially if you add a sprinkle of sweetener powder on top. They also make a good post-workout snack if you add some mixed berries on the top and it helps replenish your energy stores after a training session.

Image credit: Natasha Breen

Blueberry Pancakes

Here is an alternative recipe for pancakes that are keto-friendly, proving that pancakes really can be on the keto-breakfast menu. These are ideal for a once-a-week treat and will satisfy a sweet tooth or those moments when you crave something stodgy without disrupting your diet.

This recipe serves five people.
A serving contains just under 6 grams of carbohydrates.

Ingredients:
- 3 eggs.
- 250 grams of ricotta.
- ½ teaspoon of vanilla extract.
- 85 ml of almond milk (unsweetened).
- 340 grams of almond flour.
- 170 grams of flaxseed meal.
- 1 tablespoon of baking powder.
- ½ teaspoon of sweetener (use stevia).
- A handful of blueberries.

Method:
1 – Get the blender out and whizz up the eggs, the ricotta, the almond milk, and the vanilla extract.

2 – In a different bowl, mix the almond flour, the flaxseed meal, the stevia sweetener, and the baking powder.

3 – Add the dry ingredients to the liquid mix in the blender, adding them slowly and in bits. Keep blending bit by bit until it's all in and forms a batter. Halve the blueberries and add them in. You need about 3 blueberries per pancake so 15 blueberries in total should be enough.

4 – Melt butter into the frying pan and cook 5 pancakes until light brown.

Tip: If you are craving something sweet, these make a great sweet snack or dessert. Simply sprinkle some extra stevia on top to get a real sweet kick.

Image credit: gsk2014

THE COMPLETE KETOGENIC COOKBOOK

Breakfast Bagels

When you have that feeling for some carbs in the morning, satisfy it with these keto-friendly breakfast bagels. As it's not the quickest meal to make in the morning, it's good to make a batch of them for future use (you can freeze these). Add with bacon or smoked salmon to push your fat content even higher.

This recipe serves three people (it makes three bagels).
A serving has 5 grams of carbohydrates

Ingredients:

- Bagel:
- ¾ of an average-coffee cup of almond flour.
- 1 teaspoon of chia seeds.
- 1 large egg.
- 2 cups of shredded cheese (cheddar or parmesan is good).
- 2 tablespoons of full-fat cream cheese

  Bagel topping
- 1 tablespoon of full-fat butter
- Sesame seeds (optional)

Method:

1 – Mix the almond flour and the chia seeds together then add the egg. Mix all together until it looks like a dough.

2 – Melt the cream cheese and shredded cheese together over a pan or in the microwave.

3 – Add the two mixtures together – the dough and the cheese – and knead it until it combines.

4 – Divide the dough into 3 parts. Roll into sausages and make a bagel-like circle out of each one. Place on a baking tray and cover in the full-fat butter (melt it before) and sprinkle the seeds on top.

5 –Cook for about 15 – 20 minutes, or until golden brown. Serve warm with your choice of fillings. Smoked salmon or avocado and rocket is a great filling.

Image credit: AnikonaAnn

Spinach And Cheese Wraps

A breakfast wrap is a wonderful way to start the day, yet the average shop-bought wrap contains heaps of carbs and is not keto-friendly. So, how about this keto-friendly alternative? The wrap is made of egg and has the same texture as a regular wrap. As well as being low in carbs, it is also gluten-free and vegetarian.

This recipe serves two people.

It is gluten-free and vegetarian.

A serving contains 4 grams of carbohydrates.

Ingredients:

- 5 eggs.
- 3 egg whites.
- 1 teaspoon of sesame oil.
- A handful of fresh spinach.
- ½ cup of cheese (parmesan or cheddar is great).
- ½ cup of chopped deli ham.

Method:

1 – Mix the whole eggs, the egg whites, and the sesame oil in a bowl. Season with a pinch of salt and whisk everything together.

2 – Cook the mixture in a pan on a low heat. The wrap should be thin so cook the mixture in parts if you have a smaller pan.

3 – Gently fry the spinach leaves separately until they wilt. Take your wraps and fill with the spinach, the cheese, and the deli ham.

4 – Roll the wraps up and they're ready to eat!

Tip: Wrap in paper to take out with you as a snack. For breakfast, serve with a side of sliced avocado to add extra fat content.

Image credit: Little Hand Creations

Savoury Waffles

If you thought waffles were off the keto-menu, think again. With less than 4 grams of carbohydrates per serving, they are a low-carb way to start the day. Serve with sliced avocado to get the fat content even higher and get your metabolism into a fat-burning mode.

This recipe makes 12 waffles.

A serving (in other words, a waffle) contain 3.5 grams of carbohydrates.

Ingredients:

- 450 grams of coconut flour.
- 3 teaspoons of baking powder.
- 1 teaspoon of dried sage.
- ½ teaspoon of garlic powder (add more or less depending on your taste).
- 680 ml of coconut milk.
- 170 ml of water (or half a cup).
- 2 eggs.
- 3 tablespoons of coconut oil.
- 340 grams of shredded cheese (cheddar or parmesan).

Method:

1 – Mix the flour, the baking powder, the sage, the garlic, and a pinch of salt.

2 – Add the coconut milk, water, and coconut oil and mix. Then mix in the cheese.

3 – Grease the waffle maker and pour in enough mixture for one waffle.

4 – Each waffle-maker has its own time to cook so keep an eye on them. They will be ready when they are golden-brown.

Tip: Serve with a dollop of butter or fruit for a sweet dessert.

Image credit: Volodyer

Sausage Casserole

This is a hearty meal for the day and will set you up for the whole morning. It's a breakfast meal although it could be used as a light lunch served with an avocado salad too. It's high in fat and low in carbs so a great morning meal.

This recipe serves six people.
A serving contains 4 grams of carbohydrates.

Ingredients:

- 28 grams of sausage (pork sausage without any added sugar. Organic is ideal).
- 500 grams of chopped zucchini.
- 500 grams of shredded green cabbage.
- 170 grams of chopped onion.
- 3 eggs.
- 170 grams of mayonnaise.
- 2 teaspoons of yellow mustard.
- 1 teaspoon of ground sage.
- 400 grams of shredded cheese (cheddar or parmesan).
- A sprinkle of salt and cayenne pepper.

Method:

1 - Take the sausage meat out of the skin and cook until golden brown.

2 – Add the cabbage, onion, and zucchini. Cook until the sausage is totally cooked and the vegetables are soft.

3 – Take the sausage and vegetables out and put into a casserole dish.

4 – In a separate bowl, mix the eggs, mayonnaise, mustard, sage, and pepper together. Add in the cheese, but leave a bit to sprinkle on top after.

5 – Pour all this lovely mixture into the casserole dish. Then sprinkle the remaining cheese on top.

6 – Cook for about 30 minutes.

Tip: Add a sprinkle of parsley on top for extra taste.

Image credit: Africa Studio.

Lemon And Poppy Seed Muffins

Once again, muffins are on the menu and this time, they are sweet! Not only are they delicious, but they also have very few carbs which make them an ideal breakfast choice. They are also relatively high in fat, but you can add extra fat by drinking your morning coffee with some full-fat cream. Lemon and poppy seed muffins taste amazing with a creamy coffee.

This recipe makes 12 muffins.

Each serving (in other words, one muffin) contains under 2 grams of carbohydrates.

Ingredients:

- 250 grams of almond flour.
- 80 grams of flaxseed meal.
- 110 grams of sweetener (erythritol is a wonderful choice).
- 1 teaspoon of baking powder.
- 2 tablespoons of poppy seeds.
- 80 grams of butter (full-fat and melted).
- 80 grams of full-fat cream.
- 3 eggs.
- Lemon zest from 2 lemons.
- 3 tablespoons of lemon juice.
- 1 teaspoon of vanilla extract.
- A few drops of liquid stevia sweetener (about 20 drops is fine).

Method:

1 – Mix the flaxseed meal, the almond flour, the poppy seeds, and the erythritol sweetener all together in a bowl.

2 – Then add the eggs, melted butter, and cream. Mix until smooth.

3 – Add the liquid stevia, vanilla extract, baking powder, the lemon zest, and the lemon juice, mixing everything.

4 – Divide the mixture into 12 muffin or cupcake cases.

5 – Cook for about 20 minutes before taking them out the oven and leaving to cool.

Tip: These can also be a great afternoon snack, especially to accompany your afternoon coffee if you have one.

Image credit: CaseyMartin

Coconut Porridge

Porridge with oats is out of the conversation on the keto diet, yet there are delicious alternatives such as this coconut porridge that will give you the satisfaction of a hot, filling meal but with few carbs. It is also high in fat, helping to kick-start your body fat-burning mode and keep you feeling full throughout the morning.

This recipe serves one person.
A serving has 4 grams of carbohydrates.

Ingredients:

- 30 grams of butter (pure, full-fat).
- 1 egg.
- 1 tablespoon of coconut flour (organic if possible).
- 1 teaspoon of flaxseeds.
- 5 tablespoons of coconut cream.
- Salt to taste.

Method:

1 – Put everything in a saucepan together and mix over a low heat. It will eventually begin to thicken and is ready when you get the texture you like the most.

2 – Put in a bowl and add some extra coconut cream. If you fancy an extra bit of sweet, serve with a couple of blackberries, blueberries, cranberries, or some almonds for some extra fat.

Image credit: Vladislave Noseek

Pumpkin Spice Latte

For those mornings when we just can't stomach food but want a coffee, this pumpkin spice latte will hit the spot. High in fat and low in carbs, it provides a surprisingly filling way to start the day and will keep you going for a couple of hours. It's extra yummy on a cold wintry morning or can even be a late afternoon snack by itself.

This recipe serves three people.
A serving contains 2.5 grams of carbohydrates.

Ingredients:

- 2 cups of freshly brewed coffee.
- 340 grams (or one cup) of coconut milk.
- 80 grams (about a quarter of a cup) of pumpkin puree (unsweetened with no added sugar).
- 1 tablespoon of pumpkin pie spice blend*.
- ½ teaspoon of cinnamon.
- 1 teaspoon of vanilla extract.
- 2 tablespoons of full-fat cream.
- 2 tablespoons of butter.
- 10 drops of stevia liquid sweetener.

*If you want to make your own pumpkin pie spice blend, mix 2 tablespoons of ground cinnamon, 1 tablespoon of ground ginger, ½ teaspoon of allspice, ½ teaspoon of ground nutmeg, ½ teaspoon of ground cloves, and ¼ teaspoon of cardamom.

Method:

1 – Add the pumpkin puree, the coconut milk, the butter, and the spices to a pan over a low heat. Mix together and at the same time, start brewing your favorite coffee.

2 – Add the coffee to the pumpkin mix and stir well.

3 – Add the drops of stevia sweetener and then the full-fat cream. Mix everything well, using a handheld blender if necessary.

4 – Pour into a couple of glasses, add some extra whipped cream, and sprinkle with some extra pumpkin spice on top.

Image credit: Brent Hofacker

Chapter Summary:

In this chapter, we looked at 15 different breakfast recipes that are ideal for a keto-friendly meal to start the day.

- Your fat-burning enzymes are most active in the morning which is why it is great to start the day with a high fat and very low carb meal.

- Eggs are one of the most popular choices for breakfast on the keto diet, and the varieties of ways you can cook them are endless. However, for those that don't like eggs, there are plenty of other breakfast options available too.

- We looked at several different recipes, including keto substitutes to old-time favorites such as wraps, muffins, bagels, and waffles.

In the next chapter, we will look at some great lunch options that will help you stay on track with your keto diet.

Chapter Two: Lunch Recipes For Keto Dieting

In this chapter, we will be looking at some lunch recipes that are ideal for the keto-diet.

We saw in the last chapter that our fat-burning enzymes are at their most effective in the morning when we wake up. Therefore, it is good to start the day with a high-fat and very low carb content meal. For lunch, it's good to continue with a similar theme with meals that are high in fat and low in carbs to keep the fat-burning going. Let's look at some easy and delicious keto lunch options.

In this chapter, we'll look at the following recipes (in order):

- Smoked salmon salad.
- Chicken breast and avocado salad.
- Ham, blue cheese, and pear salad.
- T-bone steak with vegetables.
- Minced beef with broccoli.
- Sausage with mash.
- Alternative keto 'lasagna'.
- Italian cheese bread.
- BLT sandwich.
- Flourless pizza.
- Chicken casserole.
- Frittata with spinach.
- Keto meatballs.
- Prosciutto wrapped asparagus with goat's cheese.
- Quesadillas

Smoked Salmon Salad

Pressed for time? Then this salad is a perfect choice for a quick, on-the-go option that is both satisfying and delicious. It has very few carbs so it can be enjoyed guilt-free.

This recipe serves two people.
A serving contains 2 grams of carbohydrates.

Ingredients:

- 340 grams of smoked salmon.
- 55 grams of spinach.
- 1 avocado.
- Half a cucumber sliced.
- 1 tablespoon of olive oil.
- ½ a lime.
- Mayonnaise (optional).
- Salt and pepper to taste.

Method:

1 – Shred the smoked salmon and mix with the spinach, sliced avocado, and the cucumber.

2 – Squeeze lime juice over the salad, drizzle the olive oil, add a pinch of salt and pepper, and add an additional dollop of mayonnaise if you want.

Tip: Add in a few rocket leaves for a slightly spicy taste.

Image credit: bitt24

Chicken Breast And Avocado Salad

White meat such as chicken goes well with avocado and makes a satisfying meal. Serve with a salad to get some extra nutrients and make it more filling while keeping carbs low.

This recipe serves two people.
A serving contains 4 grams of carbohydrates.

Ingredients:

- 500 grams of chicken breast.
- 1 avocado.
- 2 tablespoons of full-fat butter.
- Sesame seeds (as many as you like to sprinkle on top of the chicken).
- A handful of rocket leaves.
- A few cherry tomatoes halved.
- Salt and pepper to taste.
- A sprinkle of olive oil (to dress the rocket and avocado).

Method:

1 – Add the chicken breasts to a pan and cook in the butter on a low heat. Cook each side until golden brown. Prick the chicken to test that it's cooked – if clear liquid runs out, it's cooked. Sprinkle sesame seeds on top of the chicken when it's nearly cooked to give it an extra texture.

2 – Put the rocket leaves and the halved cherry tomatoes on a plate with the slices of avocado. Sprinkle with some olive oil, some salt, and a bit of pepper before serving the chicken on top.

Tip: You can swap the rocket leaves for kale or spinach if you prefer. Also, the sesame seeds can be replaced with your favorite seed or even just cooked without any seeds at all.

Image credit: Elena Shashkina

Ham, Blue Cheese, And Pear Salad

This refreshing salad is perfect for a light yet filling lunch option. The additional walnuts and blue cheese add in extra fat and keep you full for longer. The lunch is low-carb too so is very keto-friendly.

This recipe is for two people.
Each serving has 4 grams of carbohydrates.

Ingredients:

- 130 grams of deli ham slices.
- 20 grams of walnuts (chop in half).
- 1 teaspoon of water.
- 1 tablespoon of stevia sweetener.
- 40 grams of blue cheese (if you don't like blue cheese, you can replace this with parmesan).
- ½ a small pear.
- 60 grams of mixed green leaves – like spinach, rocket, and lettuce.

For the dressing:

- 2 tablespoons of white wine vinegar.
- 2 teaspoons of olive oil.
- ½ teaspoon of wholegrain mustard.
- ½ teaspoon of Dijon mustard.

Method:

1 – Caramelise your walnuts by adding the water to a frying pan with the stevia sweetener and frying the walnuts in the mix. After a couple of minutes, take the mix out of the frying pan and put on a plate. Tip: do not touch the walnuts at this stage as they will be piping hot!

2 – Chop the ham, cheese, and pear into cubes and mix with the green leaves. Then add the walnuts on top.

3 – Mix all the ingredients for the dressing together and pour all over your side. Sprinkle with salt for taste.

Image credit: zefirchik06

T-Bone Steak With Vegetables

Sometimes, the simplest lunches are the best ones as this T-bone steak shows. This recipe is designed for you to make at home but it also gives you an idea of the kind of meals you can eat if you are eating out on the go. Red meat is preferred on the keto-diet as it is high in fat and lower in carbs than white meat. This lunch will take just a few minutes to cook, and the heavy red meat should help you stay full till dinner.

This recipe served one person.

A serving contains 4 grams of carbohydrates.

Ingredients:

- 350 grams of T-bone steak.
- 2 tablespoons of butter.
- A handful of spinach.
- ½ carrot peeled and sliced.
- Salt and pepper to taste.

Method:

1 – Boil the carrot until soft and then fry gently in a tablespoonful of butter with the spinach until the spinach starts to wilt.

2 – Take the vegetables out and serve on a plate. Leave the butter in there and add the remaining tablespoon. Place the T-bone steak in the pan, season it, and cook on both sides until cooked the way you like it.

3 – Serve the steak with the vegetables.

Tip: Feeling really hungry? Serve this with a fried egg or half an avocado.

Image credit: Farbled

Chunky Beef With Broccoli

Looking for something quick and simple? This recipe is ideal. It is also a great lunch option for those on a keto diet yet still work out as the basic ingredients help build muscles and keep you lean.

This recipe serves two people.
A serving has 5 grams of carbohydrates.

Ingredients:

- 350 grams of beef chunks (try to get a version that is as fatty as possible).
- 85 grams of full-fat butter.
- 250 grams of broccoli.
- Salt and pepper to taste.
- 150 grams of mayonnaise (optional).

Method:

1 – Take apart the broccoli by taking the heads off and chopping up the stems.

2 – Add about two-thirds of the butter to the pan and start frying the meat and the broccoli together. Season with salt and pepper.

3 – Once the meat is cooked, take it out and put on a plate. Add the rest of the butter and fry the broccoli a bit more.

4 – Take the broccoli off the heat and serve with the beef. Pour over the butter from the frying pan onto the meat. If you want, add the mayonnaise on top of the beef.

Tip: mix in chopped garlic to the butter for an extra, delicious taste. Also, you can sprinkle the broccoli with chili flakes to add some heat. For an extra crunch, sprinkle over some sesame seeds. You can also switch between minced beef and chunks of beef.

Image credit: Vladyslav Rasulov

Sausage With Mash

This alternative take on the classic sausage with mashed potatoes brings high-quality sausages with a substitute for mash – creamy shredded cabbage which has a great taste and similar texture to the mashed potato. Of course, this meal doesn't have the same amount of carbs as its regular potato version does and still has a high-fat content. The key to this meal is to get the highest quality sausage you can find and make sure that there is no added sugar or additives. If you can buy them local and organic, even better.

This recipe serves four people.
A serving has 12 grams of carbohydrates.

Ingredients:

- 680 grams of sausage. You can use chorizos, farmhouse sausages, or anything you like. Just make sure it is fresh, organic (if possible), and free from sugar.
- 2 tablespoons of full-fat butter.
- 650 grams of cabbage (green is the best).
- 55 grams of butter.
- 420 grams of full-fat whipping cream.
- The zest of half a lemon.
- A bunch of fresh parsley chopped up.
- Salt and pepper to taste.

Method:

1 – Cook the sausage in the butter. Frying it is the best way.

2 – As that's cooking, shred the cabbage (you can use a knife or even whizz it through the food processor).

3 – Fry the cabbage on high heat in the butter left over from cooking the sausages. The cabbage is ready when it is a light golden brown.

4 – Adding the whipping cream to the cabbage. Mix and let the cream come to a boil before reducing the heat and allowing the cream to reduce and become thicker. Season with salt and pepper to please your taste.

5 – Serve the sausages and cabbage on a plate and add a sprinkle of parsley and lemon zest.

Image credit: Sebastian Studio

Alternative Keto 'Lasagna'

Not quite lasagne, yet the perfect keto alternative. Instead of layers of high carb pasta, this calls for layers of high-fat, delicious deli beef. The meal is low in carbs yet extremely satisfying, keeping you full until your mid-afternoon snack. It is also very easy to make, and the fact that you make it inside a small dish means you can take it with you if you are out and about all day.

This recipe serves one person.
Each serving has 4 grams of carbohydrates.

Ingredients:

- 60 grams of deli beef slices (get the roast beef).
- 1 tablespoon of sour cream (full-fat).
- 2 tablespoons of green chilies chopped up.
- 45 grams of shredded cheese (mozzarella or parmesan).
- Some smoked paprika for the topping (optional).

Method:

1 – Piece the beef slices into smaller bits. Layer the ramekin with the beef bits until it covers the bottom.

2 – Then add a layer of a ½ tablespoon of sour cream followed by a ½ tablespoon of the green chilies.

3 – Then add about a third of the cheese.

4. Repeat this until all the ingredients are used up and you have several layers.

5. Pop into the microwave to melt the cheese. Serve with a sprinkle of paprika.

Image credit: Photomontage

Italian Cheese Bread

All the satisfaction of bread with fewer carbs. This Italian cheese bread will keep you feeling full through the whole of mid-day all the way to dinner and it has the texture of bread, while still being good for your keto-diet. It's good to make this in a large batch so you can keep some aside for a snack later or even have it for breakfast or for lunch the next day. The beauty of this bread is that it is so easy to make and doesn't take long at all.

This recipe is for four people.
One serving has 3 grams of carbohydrates.

Ingredients:

- 420 grams of shredded cheese (cheddar or parmesan).
- 1 egg.
- 1 egg yolk.
- 4 tablespoons of coconut flour.
- 3 tablespoons of flaxseed meal.
- 55 grams of Italian salami.
- 55 grams of provolone cheese (or any kind of smoked cheese).
- 1 teaspoon of Italian seasoning.
- 30 grams of spinach.
- 80 grams of mild peppers chopped.
- 1 teaspoon of olive oil.

Method:

1 – Mix the flaxseed meal, the coconut flour, and the seasoning. Then, in another bowl, melt the shredded cheese. Melting it in the microwave will be fine too.

2 – Mix the egg with the cheese. Then gradually add the dry ingredients from step one into the eggy-cheese mix until it becomes a

dough.

3 – Roll out onto parchment paper and then spread out the salami and provolone in the middle. Then add the spinach on top and the chopped peppers.

4 – Cut the sides of the dough into strips and pull them into the center. You are essentially 'braiding' your bread.

5 – Spread the egg yolk over the top and then bake for about 20 minutes. Once cooked, divide into four and eat.

Tip: You can try substituting the coconut flour with almond flour for a different taste or trying different cheeses if you like. You can also add in sundried tomatoes instead of spinach and throw in a few basil leaves. Making little tweaks like this will make a difference and won't affect the carb content.

Image credit: Danilova Janna

BLT Sandwich

One thing that many people miss on the keto diet is bread. This BLT sandwich contains a keto-friendly bread that tastes like the real deal and yet has far fewer carbs. This recipe is for a BLT, but you can swap it for other fillings. It's a great lunch option to keep your motivation levels high and to stop you from feeling you are missing out on certain foods.

This recipe serves four people.
A serving has 4 grams of carbohydrates.

Ingredients:

For the bread:
- 3 eggs.
- 130 grams of cream cheese.
- ½ tablespoon of ground psyllium husk powder (you can buy this at health stores or online).
- ½ teaspoon of baking powder.

For the filling:
- 140 grams of bacon.
- 55 grams of lettuce.
- 1 finely sliced tomato.
- 8 tablespoons of mayonnaise.
- A few sprigs of fresh basil.

Method:

1 – Start by dividing your eggs so you have the whites in one bowl and then put the yolks into a different bowl.

2 – Mix the whites with a pinch of salt until they become stiff.

3 – Add the cream cheese to the egg yolks and mix well. Then add the psyllium seed husk and the baking powder. These will give the bread a more bread-like texture.

4 – Now you need to add the whites to the yolk. To do this, you need to fold the whites into the yolk, keeping as much air in the whites as possible.

5 – Divide the mixture into eight parts and pop them on a baking tray. Then bake for about 25 minutes. They should look golden brown when they are ready.

6 – Now your bread is done, the next part is to make the BLT. Start by frying the bacon.

7 – While the bacon is cooking, spread the mayonnaise over the bread. Then add the lettuce, the tomato, the cooked bacon, and a few sprigs of basil leaves.

Image credit: Emilie Bourdages.

Flourless Pizza

Keto-diets even include pizza. This pizza strays away from the regular pizza as its base is made entirely from chicken meat. The base still has a kind of doughy texture, so it almost feels like you are getting a regular pizza. The taste is delicious and not only that; it is very low in carbs so can be eaten practically guilt-free.

This recipe serves eight people.

A serving has less than 1 gram of carbohydrates, making this a great dish for when you're feeling extra hungry. A small binge on this pizza shouldn't affect your ketosis state.

Ingredients:

- 450 grams of chicken thighs. Get the ones that are skinless and boneless.
- 340 grams of mozzarella (get the full-fat kind).
- 1 egg.
- 30 grams of blue cheese (crumble it or finely chop it).
- 1 teaspoon of oregano.
- Salt and pepper to taste.
- 2 tablespoons of butter.
- 1 tablespoon of sour cream.
- 3 tablespoons of chili sauce (make sure it has no added sugar).
- 1 sprig of celery.
- A handful of rocket.

Method:

1 - Blend the chicken thigh meat in a blender until it's in small pieces.

2 – Pop the chicken in a bowl and then add half of the mozzarella, the

oregano, salt and pepper to your taste, and the egg. Mix everything.

3 – Spread the mix on a pizza tray and roll it out until it's about ¼ inch thick. Then put in the oven and cook for about 20 minutes or until it's golden brown and a little bit crispy.

4 – As the crust cooking is going on, melt the butter and add the chopped celery until it goes a bit brown.

5 – In a different bowl, mix the sour cream with the chili sauce.

6 – Take the crust out of the oven, smother it with the sour cream sauce, sprinkle the celery over the top, then add the rest of the mozzarella and the blue cheese.

7 – Finally, put it back in the oven to melt the cheese. To garnish, add the rocket leaves and some extra lashings of chili sauce if you like it hot.

Image credit: Prostock-studio

THE COMPLETE KETOGENIC COOKBOOK

Chicken Casserole

This delicious casserole brings the taste of the Mediterranean with low carbs and plenty of taste. It's a great dish to make in batches and save for a few days (you can freeze it as well). The rich combination of ingredients will keep you satisfied, and its low carb and high-fat content will keep you full for the afternoon.

This recipe serves four people.
A serving has 7 grams of carbohydrates.

Ingredients:

- 700 grams of chicken (it can be breast or thighs, whatever you prefer).
- 55 grams of butter.
- 85 grams of pesto. You can use green or red pesto, whatever you prefer.
- 400 grams of full-fat cream.
- A handful of black olives (without the stone).
- 230 grams of feta cheese.
- 1 or 2 garlic cloves chopped.
- Salt and pepper to taste.
- A handful of mixed, green leaves.

Method:

1 – Cut the chicken into pieces and fry in the butter.

2 – While the chicken is cooking, mix the cream and the pesto in a bowl.

3 – Once the chicken is cooked, put it in a baking dish and mix with

olives, feta cheese (sprinkle it evenly over the chicken) and sprinkle the garlic all over the chicken too.

4 – Then pour over the pesto mixture.

5 – Cook for about 30 minutes until it's bubbling slightly on the edges.

Image credit: Magrig

Frittata With Spinach

This frittata is great for several reasons. First, it's easy to make and doesn't take too long to make either. Secondly, you can make a batch of them and use them not only as a lunch option but as an on-the-go snack. Thirdly, they are filling and will keep hunger at bay. Finally, they are high in fat and low in carbs, perfect for your keto-diet.

This recipe serves four people.
A serving contains 4 grams.

Ingredients:

- 8 eggs.
- 340 grams of full-fat cream.
- 250 grams of spinach.
- 150 grams of chorizo (or cooked bacon). Dice it into small bits.
- 150 grams of shredded cheese (parmesan is an excellent choice).
- 2 tablespoons of butter.
- Salt and pepper to taste.

Method:

1 – Fry the chorizo and the spinach together in the butter.

2 – Mix the eggs with the cream and pour the mixture into a baking dish.

3 – Add the bacon and spinach before sprinkling the cheese on the top.

4 – Cook for about 30 minutes until it is firm and the cheese has melted and started to turn brown.

Tip: Serve with a salad of chopped avocado and a drizzle of oil with a sprinkle of chili flakes for an even more satisfying meal.

Image credit: Brent Hofacker

Keto Meatballs

These delicious meatballs make a quick lunch for when you are after something light and easy. You can make several batches in advance to pack for lunch and take with you or eat later. Couple of these will make an ideal, keto-friendly snack and the high proteins and fats will ward off hunger until your next meal.

This recipe serves four people.
A serving contains 1 gram of carbohydrates.

Ingredients:

- 680 grams of ground beef.
- 2 tablespoons of full-fat butter.
- 110 grams of grated cheese (cheddar or parmesan is great).
- 100 grams of mayonnaise.
- 4 tablespoons of pickled jalapenos.
- 1 tablespoon of chili powder (or paprika if you prefer).
- 1 tablespoon of Dijon mustard.
- Salt, pepper, and cayenne pepper to taste.

Method:

1 – Mix the mayonnaise, the jalapenos, the chili powder, the Dijon mustard, the cayenne pepper, the cheddar cheese, and add a hint of salt and pepper.

2 – Once well mixed, add the ground beef.

3 – Mix and create meatballs from the mix.

4 – Fry them in butter until cooked all the way through.

Tip: Serve with a simple avocado side. Mix half an avocado with mayonnaise, a hint of lime juice, some chopped garlic, and some salt.

Image credit: zefirchik06

Prosciutto Wrapped Asparagus With Goat's Cheese

The flavor may be something quite sophisticated, yet this is so easy to make and takes hardly any time. It's an ideal light lunch and can be easily taken out with you when you on the road. You can eat this pretty much guilt-free as each serving has just one gram of carbs.

This recipe serves four people.

Each serving has 1 gram of carbohydrates (a serving is three sticks of asparagus so you can triple this and still have a low carb count).

Ingredients:

- 12 sticks of green asparagus.
- 55 grams of prosciutto. Get the ones in slices.
- 140 grams of goat's cheese.
- 2 tablespoons of olive oil.
- Black pepper and salt to taste.

Method:

1 – After washing the asparagus, slice the goat's cheese into 12 slices. Then, divide those 12 slices into two parts.

2 – Next, slice the prosciutto into two pieces lengthways. Then wrap two prosciutto pieces and two cheese pieces around one asparagus.

3 – Put all the wrapped asparagus in a baking dish and drizzle with olive oil and salt and pepper.

4 – Cook in the oven for about 15 minutes. If you like them crispy, leave for longer. If you prefer asparagus soft, then parboil the asparagus before putting the ham and cheese on and bake them in the oven for less time.

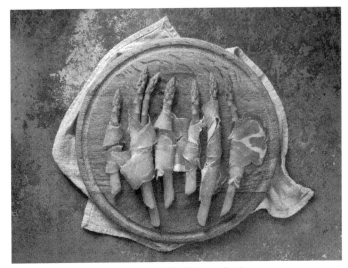

Image credit: Fortyforks

Quesadillas

Light yet satisfying, these quesadillas are not only high in fat and low in carbs, but they are also vegetarian. If you want to make it meaty, you can add in chunks of chicken or beef and adjust the carb content accordingly. Whether you get them with or without meat, they are delicious and can be easily wrapped up and taken out with you for a lunch on-the-go.

This recipe serves three people.
Each serving contains 5 grams of carbohydrates.

Ingredients:

For the tortillas:
- 2 eggs
- 2 egg whites.
- 170 grams of cream cheese.
- 1 and ½ tablespoons of ground psyllium husk powder (or you can use flaxseed meal).
- 1 tablespoon of coconut flour (or, try almond flour).
- Salt to taste.

For the filling:
- 140 grams of grated cheese (cheddar is fine, or any hard cheese).
- A bunch of leafy greens such as spinach, rocket, and lettuce.
- 1 tablespoon of olive oil.

Method:

1 – Mix the eggs and the egg whites together. Add the cream cheese and mix until the mixture is perfectly smooth. You can do this with a fork or just pop it all into a mixer.

2 – In a different bowl, mix the salt, the coconut flour, and the psyllium husk powder. Gradually add this dry mixture into the egg mixture from the first step. Keep mixing the egg mix as you're doing it. Let it set a little while and mix again. It will eventually get the consistency of a pancake mixture.

3 – Create six tortilla circles on a baking tray and cook for about 5 minutes. Keep an eye on them. Once they look golden brown, they're done.

4 – Now you have the tortillas, it is time to make your quesadillas. Take three tortillas and divide half the grated cheese between them.

5 – Then, add the leafy greens on top of the cheese, add the rest of the cheese, and then add another tortilla on top.

6 – Fry each quesadilla in a frying pan with butter until the cheese melts.

Tip: The most delicious sides you can serve with these quesadillas are guacamole or sour cream. You can make your own guacamole with avocado, chopped onion, garlic, jalapenos, chili, and tomato before mixing it all together with some parsley and lime juice. You can also mix in some mayonnaise too. Sour cream you can buy from the store. Make sure to look for full-fat and check it has no added sugar.

Image credit: EQRoy

Chapter Summary:

In this chapter, we looked at some great keto-friendly recipes that you can cook for lunch.

- At lunchtime, your enzymes are still active and continue to be in a fast-paced fat burning mode. It is good to have a high-fat lunch with fewer carbs to keep your metabolism going.

- We looked at fifteen different meals including alternatives for classics such as pizza, sandwiches, and bread.

- There are so many alternatives and substitutes for high carb ingredients that it's easy to eat regular food that is low-carb and high fat. It pays to prepare in advance and cook lunches for the week ahead to help avoid making the wrong food choices when you are outside of the home.

In the next chapter, we will look at some keto-friendly dinner recipes.

Chapter Three: Keto Dinner Recipes

In this chapter, we will be looking at great dinner recipes to eat while on the keto diet.

At the end of the day, your enzymes are at their least active and won't be burning fat as quickly as they were at the start of the day. Dinner should be something healthy and relatively light, so your body isn't digesting a huge meal throughout the night. It is always work remembering that while counting a low carb level is important, don't overdo it on the calories. Many people are prone to snacking in the evening so keep focused on having just one good, keto-friendly meal.

In this chapter, we will look at the following meals:

- Baked Italian meatballs.
- Beef Wellington.
- Roast beef easy cheddar salad.
- Rib-eye steak with vegetables.
- Keto nachos.
- Roast chicken
- Chicken garam masala.
- Chicken Caesar salad
- Pork stir fry.
- Salmon with avocado.
- Pan-fried salmon with asparagus.
- Fish coconut curry.
- Salad niçoise
- Mushroom omelet.
- Fried eggs with pork and kale

Baked Italian Meatballs

Keto dieting can sometimes seem restrictive, and it is normal to miss filling homemade foods such as large, carb-loaded Italian dishes. While carbs are off the menu, Italian doesn't have to be, and these meatballs show that you can still have comfort food during keto dieting. Using natural ingredients, these meatballs are healthy and low in carbs.

This recipe serves four people.
A serving has 8 grams of carbohydrates.

Ingredients:

- 450 grams of minced beef.
- 1 tablespoon of oregano and thyme mixed together.
- 800 grams of tomatoes (whole and peeled).
- Half a red onion finely chopped.
- Two crushed garlic cloves.
- 1 tablespoon of tomato paste
- 170 grams of grated cheddar, parmesan, or mozzarella.
- Salt and pepper to taste.
- A few sprigs of fresh basil.

Method:

1 – Mix the beef, the thyme and oregano, and the salt and pepper in a bowl.

2 – Divide this mixture into 16 balls.

3 – Cook the meatballs in butter in a frying pan until nicely browned.

4 – Take the meatballs out and save a tablespoon of the juices. Then add the tinned tomatoes, the onion, the tomato paste, and the garlic into the same pan. Mix everything together, break the tomatoes down into smaller bits, and stir until the sauce has thickened.

5 – Put the meatballs into a baking dish, pour over the tomato sauce, and then sprinkle the cheese over the top.

6 – Cook for about 20 minutes with foil wrapped over the dish. Then, take off the foil and cook for another 5 minutes to let the cheese go brown and a bit crispy.

7 – Let it cool down a bit and serve with a sprinkle of fresh basil leaves.

Image credit: Piotr Krzeslak

Beef Wellington

This is the perfect dinner when you want to cook something fancy, delicious, yet keto-friendly. A popular item on many restaurants menus, this one here is the low-carb version. Typically, the beef wellington is hard to get exactly right, yet this recipe is pretty straightforward and easy to make.

This recipe serves four people.
Each serving contains 3 grams of carbohydrates.

Ingredients:

- 2 large tenderloin steaks cut in half to make four equal bits.
- 1 tablespoon of butter.
- Salt and pepper to taste.
- 1 cup of grated cheese (parmesan is fine).
- 170 grams of almond flour.
- 4 tablespoons of liver pate.

Method:

1 – Sprinkle salt and pepper on your steaks, melt the butter in a frying pan, and put the steaks in. Do this on a high heat.

2 – Cook each side for about 2 minutes to thoroughly sear each side. Take them from the frying pan and let them cool.

3 – Next, melt the cheese in the microwave for about 1 minute or so. Then stir in the almond flour.

4 – Spread this cheesy dough on a baking tray and roll it out, using a piece of parchment paper on top of the dough to act as a barrier between the dough and the rolling pin.

5 – Put a dollop of pate on the dough and cut the dough later enough to contain the meat.

6 – Put the meat on top of the pate and wrap the dough around it.

7 – Cook for about 25 minutes or until the pastry starts to turn a golden-brown color. You can spread some extra butter on the top to glaze the pastry.

Tip: serve with a large salad of mixed green leaves tossed with olive oil, a squeeze of lime juice, and a little bit of salt.

Image credit: A_Lein

Roast Beef Easy Cheddar Salad

The thing about dinner is that sometimes we just want something instantly ready, especially after a busy day. This roast beef easy cheddar salad is simple to put together, has a healthy fat content, low carbs, and low calories as well. The cheddar cheese will help keep you satisfied and keep you away from the junk food before going to bed.

This recipe serves two people.
Each serving contains 6 grams of carbohydrates.

Ingredients:

- 200 grams of roast beef straight from the deli.
- 140 grams of cheddar cheese (get organic, unprocessed cheese, the stronger, the better).
- 1 avocado.
- 6 horse radishes sliced.
- 1 spring onion sliced.
- 60 grams of fresh, shredded iceberg lettuce.
- 170 grams of mayonnaise.
- 1 tablespoon of Dijon mustard.
- A dash of olive oil.
- Salt and pepper to taste.

Method:

1 – Put the roast beef, the avocado (sliced), the cheese, and the radishes on a plate.

2 – Add the spring onion over the top and a dollop of mustard and mayonnaise.

3- Add the lettuce and drizzle with olive oil.

4 – Optional: You can also serve it with a ripe vine tomato and a little bit of balsamic vinegar.

Tip: You can switch the roast beef for deli ham to make a change and serve with pickled onions. If you use pickled onion, check that there is no added sugar.

Image credit: Duplass

Rib-Eye Steak With Vegetables

The perfect comfort food, this rib-eye steak with vegetables is not only easy to do but also a filling, dinner option. The anchovy butter that it is served with can be made in copious quantities to use on other meats on other days. This low in carb meal is also a good option for those on a weight loss keto diet.

This recipe serves four people.
Each serving has 7 grams of carbohydrates.

Ingredients:

- 450 grams of broccoli.
- 1 whole garlic.
- 280 grams of cherry tomatoes.
- A drizzle of olive oil.
- 1 tablespoon of thyme, basil, or oregano (whichever you prefer). Used dried.
- 680 grams of rib-eye steaks.
- Salt and pepper to taste.

For the anchovy butter:
- 30 grams of anchovies.
- 140 grams of butter.
- Half a lemon for its juice.
- Salt and pepper to taste.

Method:

1 – Start by making the anchovy butter. Chop the anchovy fillets and put them together with the butter, the salt, the pepper, and the lemon juice. Give it a good mix and leave to one side.

2 – Using a roasting pan, put all the vegetables inside and drizzle with a splash of olive oil and seasoning. Also, add the garlic (unpeeled). Roast for about 15 minutes.

3 – Fry the meat at an elevated temperature in olive oil. Aim to sear the outside of the meat. Make sure you season it before frying.

4 – Put the meat in with the vegetables, lower the heat, and roast for another 15 minutes (or less if you like your meat pinker).

5 – Take from the oven and put on a plate. Serve with the anchovy butter on top of the steak.

Image credit: 54613

Keto Nachos

One of the hardest things about following the keto diet is when others around you are not on a keto diet. This meal is a version of keto nachos with low carbs. The chips are replaced with cauliflower so they are much more keto-friendly. This version alone will be satisfying, and great alternative for normal nachos. Dishes like these really make keto much easier to follow when you feel like you are eating the same foods as everyone else.

This recipe makes 5 servings.
Each serving contains 6 grams of carbohydrates.

Ingredients:

- 225 grams of sliced beef.
- 1 tablespoon of full-fat butter.
- 110 grams of coconut oil.
- 1 teaspoon of chili powder.
- ½ teaspoon of turmeric.
- 800 grams of cauliflower.
- 30 grams of grated cheese (parmesan is perfect).
- 30 grams of full-fat grated cheddar cheese.
- 30 grams of jalapeno slice.
- 110 grams of sour cream.
- 1 large avocado.

Method:

1 – Break up the head of the cauliflower.

2 – In a bowl, mix the coconut oil, the turmeric, the chili powder, and the cauliflower gently.

3 – Put the cauliflower on a baking tray, sprinkle with salt and pepper, and roast for about 25 minutes.

4 – While that's cooking, cook the steaks in butter and then allow to rest for about 5 minutes.

5 – Take the cauliflower out and put in a pan. Add the steak (slice it up first) on top of the cauliflower. Then sprinkle with cheese and jalapeno slices. Bake for about 5 minutes, so all that cheese melts nicely.

6 – Serve with guacamole, chili sauce, and sour cream.

Image credit: ES Stock

Roast Chicken

This recipe is easy to cook and keto-friendly. Serve with roasted vegetables but make sure to avoid vegetables such as potatoes or parsnips which are high in carbs. Veggies such as carrots, Brussel sprouts, and cauliflower are fine, and you can roast them too to give them extra flavor.

This recipe serves eight in total.
Each serving has 5 grams of carbohydrates.

Ingredients:

- A large fresh chicken,
- Salt and pepper.
- A handful of oregano (fresh).
- A handful of thyme (fresh).
- 1 lemon.
- 4 tablespoons of butter.
- 1 tablespoon of parsley (dried)
- Olive oil.

Method:

1 – Season the chicken with salt and pepper and stuff the cavity with the thyme and the oregano. Cut the lemon in half and pop it inside the chicken too.

2 – Tie the chicken up using twine to make sure the cavity remains sealed.

3 – Using half of the butter, spread it over the outside of the skin and add sea salt and rock black pepper on top. Then turn it over and rub in the rest of the butter and add seasoning.

4 – Roast for about 45 minutes on a low heat. Then add the parsley and spread the juices in the tray on top of the bird. Put in any vegetables you want to eat with the chicken, season, and roast for a further 40 minutes or so.

5 – Let it rest for about 10 minutes before serving it.

Tip: This is also delicious to make for a roasted lemon chicken salad. Make the roasted chicken above and serve with a bed of mixed green leaves, a drizzle of lime and olive oil, and a few slices of avocado for a light, summery dinner option.

Image credit: Brent Hofacker.

Chicken Garam Masala

This spicy dish is the ultimate comfort food when you fancy something a bit heavier. It's low in carbs and high in fats, yet watch out for the high-calorie content. This is a treat for once a week and is ideal for those Saturday nights in when you feel like spoiling yourself. If you usually order a takeaway, replace it with this for an equally satisfying meal yet one that is better for the keto diet. It is easy to make, and although the ingredients list is long, it is mostly spices that you can save for another recipe after.

This recipe serves four people.
Each serving contains 5 grams of carbohydrates.

Ingredients:

- 700 grams of organic chicken breasts.
- 3 tablespoons of butter.
- Salt to taste.
- 1 red pepper chopped up.
- 425 grams of full-fat cream.
- Some fresh parsley chopped up.

For the garam masala:
*you can buy this in the supermarket but it is better to make it from scratch. Not only is it delicious, you know exactly what is in it and avoid any added sugars.

- 1 teaspoon of ground cumin.
- 2 teaspoons of coriander seeds.
- 1 teaspoon of turmeric.
- 1 teaspoon of ginger.
- 1 teaspoon of cardamom.

- 1 teaspoon of paprika.
- 1 teaspoon of chili powder.
- A hint of ground nutmeg.

Method:

1 – Mix all the spices together.

2 – Cut the chicken breasts into slices and fry slightly.

3 – Then add in half of the spices and mix well with the chicken.

4 – Add seasoning then place the chicken with all its juices into a baking dish.

5 – In a separate bowl, mix the cream, the pepper, and the rest of spices. Spread this all over the chicken.

6 – Bake for 20 minutes and then serve with a sprinkle of parsley or a few slices of onion.

Tip: Not only is this meal gluten-free, but you can also make it dairy free too! Switch the cream for coconut cream. It's dairy-free and creates a delicious flavor to the meal. Also, swap the butter for ghee or coconut oil.

Image credit: Dinu's

Chicken Caesar Salad

This is a low carb take on the classic Caesar salad. The sauce is made from scratch, so you know exactly what it is in it. Not only is this a healthy, light salad to have for dinner, it is also great as a lunch option and can be taken out with you if you are on-the-go.

This recipe serves two people.
Each serving contains 5 grams of carbohydrates.

Ingredients:

- 340 grams of chicken breast.
- 55 grams of parmesan cheese, grated.
- ½ a whole lettuce.
- 150 grams of cooked bacon.
- Salt and pepper to taste.
- A dash of olive oil.

For the dressing:
- 170 grams of mayonnaise.
- 1 tablespoon of mustard (Dijon is delicious here).
- ½ a lemon. Use its juice and its zest.
- 2 tablespoons of parmesan cheese, grated.
- 2 tablespoons of anchovies, finely chopped.
- Salt and pepper to taste.

Method:

1 – Start with the dressing. Mix all the ingredients in a blender and leave in the fridge.

2 – Put the chicken breasts on a baking tray, drizzle with olive oil, season, and cook for about 20 minutes.

3 – Shred the lettuce and add to a plate. Cook the bacon until crispy and sprinkle over the lettuce. Then slice the chicken and then serve on top.

4 – Add the dressing and sprinkle some parmesan cheese on the top.

Image credit: Ork75

Pork Stir Fry

This quick and easy pork stir fry is served with green peppers for that added crunch. It takes just a few minutes to make and can be made in batches for the next day too. Low in carbs and relatively low in calories, it's a great dinner option for those looking to lose weight also.

This recipe serves two people.
Each serving contains 5 grams of carbohydrates.

Ingredients:

- 340 grams of pork shoulder slices.
- 2 green peppers sliced.
- 2 spring onions sliced.
- 110 grams of butter.
- 2 tablespoons almonds.
- 1 teaspoon of chili paste.
- Salt and pepper to taste.

Method:

1 –Put the butter in a frying pan (or a wok if you have one) and fry the pork, the peppers, and the spring onions. Save a bit of this butter for later for serving.

2 – Cook until the meat is brown. Add the vegetables and the chili paste and then season with salt and pepper.

3 – When it's all cooked, transfer onto a plate and serve with a dollop of butter and a sprinkle of almonds.

Tip: This recipe calls for pork, yet there are plenty of other options too. You can use strips of beef or chicken thighs. You can even use tofu to make it vegetarian or replace with the pork with peeled prawns.

Image credit: Pitiphat

Salmon With Avocado

This simple to make dish is perfect for those evenings when you do want to cook. This dish doesn't need any cooking at all and takes just a couple of minutes to prepare. The meal is low in carbs and high in good fats. Not only that, it has a relatively low-calorie content so is suitable for those on a weight loss plan.

This recipe serves two people.
Each serving contains 7 grams of carbohydrates.

Ingredients:

- 2 avocados.
- 170 grams of smoked salmon (organic if possible).
- 255 grams of crème Fraiche.
- Salt and pepper to taste.
- Half a lemon.
- A handful of mixed green leaves.

Method:

1 – Halve the avocados and take out the stone. Fill the middle of the avocado with the crème Fraiche.

2 – Add the salmon on top and season with salt and a squeeze of lemon juice.

3 – Serve with a bed of green leaves. Squeeze the rest of the lemon juice over the green leaves and add a drizzle of olive oil.

Tip: You can replace the crème Fraiche with mayonnaise if you prefer. This is best made and consumed on the same day. Otherwise, the avocado may turn brown. If the avocado turns brown, it is usually totally fine and is only less attractive as when it is all green and fresh looking, but it is still edible. You can also serve the salmon with a sprinkle of chili flakes and some additional sesame seeds for extra texture and heat.

Image credit: Vitor1

Pan-Fried Salmon With Asparagus

This recipe is super easy to make, keto-friendly, low in carbs, and relatively low in calories. It's the ideal dinner for when you want to make something quickly and easily and great for those looking to reach their weight loss goals. The salmon is a useful source of omega 3 as well.

This recipe serves two people.
Each serving has 2 grams of carbohydrates.

Ingredients:

- 225 grams of green asparagus.
- 85 grams of butter.
- 340 grams of salmon. Organic is the best if you can get it.
- Salt and pepper to taste.

Method:

1 – Put a big blob of butter in the frying pan and fry the asparagus over medium heat for about 4 minutes. Add a bit more butter and then add the salmon.

2 – Cook the salmon on both sides for a couple of minutes.

3 – Once everything is cooked, season the salmon and serve on a plate with the rest of the butter.

Tip: Dress the salmon and asparagus with a squeeze of lemon juice and a sprinkle of dill or chili flakes. You can also switch the salmon for steaks of tuna, swordfish, or other meaty fish. It's also delicious with slices of avocado, some halved cherry tomatoes, and a green salad dressed in olive oil.

Image credit: DronG

Fish Coconut Curry

This dish is easy to make, yet the taste would have people believe it's far more complicated than it is. It's keto-friendly as has few carbs and is ideal for those craving some Thai or Asian food. Leave the rice as it is loaded with carbs. It is best to eat this curry as the recipe states – it will certainly leave you full – but if you really want rice, then you can blend some parboiled cauliflower in a blender until it is in rice-sized bits. It's the healthy, non-carb version of rice yet has the same texture and very similar taste.

This recipe serves two people.

Each serving contains 5 grams of carbohydrates.

Ingredients:

- 700 grams of chunky white fish (cod is great, or anything similar).
- 30 grams of butter.
- Salt and pepper.
- 4 tablespoons of ghee.
- 2 tablespoons of red curry paste (or green if you prefer)/
- 400 grams of coconut cream (unsweetened).
- 8 tablespoons of cilantro or parsley chopped up.
- 450 grams of cauliflower.

Method:

1 – Put the fish pieces on the baking tray. Season with salt and pepper and add butter on the top.

2 – Mix the coconut cream, the chopped cilantro (or parsley), and the curry paste. Pour all over the fish.

357

3 – Bake for about 20 minutes. In the meantime, parboil the cauliflower and blend into rice-sized bits for a low-carb version of rice.

Image credit: Sta

Salad Niçoise

This light salad is packed with flavor and makes a healthy and filling dinner. It's a healthy choice, yet if you want to make it even more weight-loss friendly, then serve it with a drizzle of olive oil instead of the dressing. Either way, it is a low carb dinner option.

This recipe serves two people.
Each serving contains 13 grams of carbohydrates.

Ingredients:

- 2 eggs.
- 85 grams of celery root.
- 200 grams of green beans.
- Olive oil.
- 2 chopped garlic cloves.
- 200 grams of lettuce.
- 55 grams of cherry tomatoes.
- ½ red onion finely sliced.
- 1 can of tuna in water.
- 255 grams of black olives without the stone.
- Salt and pepper.

For the dressing:

- 30 grams of anchovies.
- 1 teaspoon of mustard (try Dijon if you can).
- 2 tablespoons of capers.
- 170 grams of olive oil.
- 4 tablespoons of mayonnaise.
- The juice of ½ a lemon.
- A sprinkle of fresh parsley.
- One garlic clove very finely chopped.

Method:

1 – Make the dressing by blending all the ingredients together. Leave to one side.

2 – Boil the eggs and let them cool when ready. Peel them and cut in half.

3 – Cut the celery root into small pieces and parboil the celery root at the same time as you're parboiling the green beans. Cook in separate pots for about 5 minutes.

4 – Take the green beans and fry on high heat in butter with seasoning and garlic.

5 – Put the lettuce on the plates and add the rest of the ingredients – the onion, the tomatoes, the tuna (remember to drain it!), the beans, the celery roots, the eggs, and the olives. Serve with the dressing poured over it or on the side.

Image credit: Elzbieta Sekowska

Mushroom Omelette

Eggs are a significant source of fat and protein for dinner just as much as they are for breakfast. This quick and easy recipe is perfect for a simple yet tasty dinner and will keep you feeling satisfied all night. It is high in good fats, low in carbs, and is ideal for those looking to lose weight. Serve it with a leafy green salad such as spinach, lettuce, and rocket, for extra nutrients. This is also a good dinner choice for vegetarians.

This recipe serves one person.
Each serving has 4 grams of carbohydrates.

Ingredients:

- 3 eggs (organic, free-range for the best taste and healthiest option).
- 30 grams of butter.
- 30 grams of grated cheese (parmesan is an excellent choice or any other kind of hard cheese).
- ¼ of an onion.
- 3 big mushrooms chopped up.
- Salt and pepper to taste.

Method:

1 – Break the eggs into a bowl. Add some salt and pepper and whisk until totally smooth.

2 – Melt butter in the frying pan and then pour in the egg mixture.

3 – When the bottom of the egg is firm, but the top is a little bit runny, sprinkle on the cheese, the onion, and the mushroom.

4 – Leave it to cook a little longer then fold it in half. It will be ready when it is golden brown.

5 – Serve hot with a nice green salad.

Tip: Add some garlic in with the butter when you are frying the mushrooms to create a garlic mushroom filling – it's delicious.

Image credit: Martin Tuzak

Fried Eggs With Pork And Kale

This dinner option is effortless to whip up and tastes delicious. It's low carb and a relatively good option for those on a weight loss diet and is excellent for those who weight train as it provides a good source of protein. Serve with a green salad with rocket, spinach, and lettuce with some halved cherry tomatoes to get a wholesome, nutritious meal.

This recipe serves two people.
Each serving contains 8 grams of carbohydrates.

Ingredients:

- 4 eggs.
- 100 grams of full-fat butter.
- 225 grams of kale.
- 225 grams of pork belly (smoked) or bacon if you can't find pork belly or only have bacon at home.
- 30 grams of walnuts.
- 4 tablespoons of cranberries.
- Salt and pepper.

Method:

1 – Cut the kale into large bits and fry in two-thirds of the butter in a frying pan. Take off the heat when the kale starts to turn brown.

2 – Take the kale out and set aside. Using the same pan, add the pork and fry until it's crispy.

3 – Then add the kale and mix in the cranberries and the nuts. Warm it all up and put in a bowl.

4 – Then fry the eggs in the same pan, adding the rest of the butter. Season and serve with the pork mix.

Image credit: Tah.suttipong

Chapter Summary

In this chapter, we looked at fifteen different dinner options that are keto-friendly. Some are simple to make in a couple of minutes and don't require cooking, whereas others are more sophisticated or great for a family meal.

- Having a satisfying dinner is vital to avoid snacking later at night.

- In this chapter, we looked at both meat and vegetarian options as well as some takes on classic dishes such as the beef wellington, coconut curry, and the chicken Caesar salad.

In the next chapter, we will see some desserts that will satisfy your sweet tooth and keep your keto diet on track.

Chapter Four: Keto Friendly Desserts

In this chapter, we will look at keto-friendly desserts.

No matter how hard we try, sometimes the craving for something sweet is too hard to ignore. Rather than craving and eating something that will jeopardize your diet, why not try one of these desserts? They are low-carb so won't flood your body with glucose and will keep your blood sugar levels balanced.

Just keep in mind that just because these desserts are low carb doesn't mean you get to eat them freely. Like most desserts, they are still high in calories so regularly eating these sweets will not help with your weight loss goals. However, to satisfy a sweet tooth or as a weekly treat, these desserts are much better for you than regular sweets that are loaded with carbohydrates and sugar.

In order, here are the desserts we will look at in this chapter.

- ☐ Oven-baked brie cheese with nuts.
- ☐ Hot chocolate.
- ☐ Chocolate mousse.
- ☐ Keto brownie.
- ☐ Pecan Chocolate.
- ☐ Coconut cream pie.
- ☐ Banana Waffles.
- ☐ Low Carb Trifle.
- ☐ Yogurt popsicles.
- ☐ Berries and whipped cream.

Oven-Baked Brie Cheese With Nuts

Whether you want a dessert post-dinner or you are having a gathering at your house and want to serve something tasty yet keto-friendly, this oven-baked brie will really hit the spot. The savory light brie goes so well with the herbs and the caramelized nuts. It's also a high in fat dessert yet very low in carbs. Cheese is also incredibly filling so eat this slowly to allow yourself time to feel full and you should stay satisfied for a good while.

This recipe serves four people.
A serving has 1 gram of carbohydrates.

Ingredients:

- 250 grams of brie. If you can't find brie, then a Camembert cheese will also work equally well.
- 55 grams of walnuts (or pecans).
- One tablespoon of water.
- 10 drops of stevia sweetener.
- 1 garlic clove.
- 1 tablespoon of rosemary (or thyme).
- 1 tablespoon of olive oil.
- Salt and pepper to taste.

Method:

1 – Pop the cheese in a non-stick baking dish. Then chop the garlic (or mince it in a garlic presser) and mix with the herbs, olive oil, and a dash of salt and pepper.

2 – Add all the chopped nuts to a frying pan with the tablespoon of water and the drops of stevia sweetener. Fry on a low heat for a couple of minutes, just enough time for the nuts to pick up the sweet

flavor. This will give the nuts a caramelized taste. Take out of the pan and leave to cool.

3 – Once cooled, add the nuts to the herb mix and spoon it on top of the cheese.

4 – Bake for about 10 minutes, letting the cheese become warm and soft.

Image credit: omaamaraa

Hot Chocolate

This hot chocolate is easy to make and low in carbs. You can make it richer and higher in fat by mixing in cream or adding whipped cream on top. It's a perfect feel-good dessert that isn't going to affect your diet negatively. Although it is suggested as a dessert, you can even make this as a breakfast drink or as a stand-alone afternoon snack.

This recipe serves one person.
A serving contains 1 gram of carbohydrates.

Ingredients:

- 70 grams of butter (full-fat, unsalted).
- 1 tablespoon of cocoa powder
- ¼ of a teaspoon of vanilla extract.
- 1 cup of boiling water.
- Whipped cream (optional).

Method:

1 – Put all the ingredients in a blender and whizz together until frothy.

Tip: If you want a milk protein-free option, use ghee or coconut oil instead of butter. If you want cream but can't tolerate dairy or just prefer to not eat dairy, then replace the cream with whipped coconut cream. It's delicious and gives it a kind of dessert taste. Chocolate and coconut can be a delightful combination. You can also sprinkle cinnamon on top.

Image credit: Julie Style

Chocolate Mousse

This chocolate mousse is a healthy take on the original by using avocado as its main ingredient. It may sound strange to put avocado and chocolate together, but the result is outstanding, especially for those with a sweet tooth. You can't taste the avocado; rather it gives the mousse a smooth, creamy texture. It's also low in carbs and high in fats, just what you want from a keto dessert.

This recipe serves one person.
There are 6 grams of carbohydrates in one serving.

Ingredients:

- ¼ cup of cocoa powder. Use a dark cocoa powder that is organic if possible.
- 1 avocado.
- 10 drops of stevia sweetener.
- ½ tablespoon of vanilla extract.
- A pinch of salt (sounds odd but it really enhances the flavor).

Method:

1 – Halve the avocado, take the stone out, and scoop the flesh into a bowl.

2 – Add the other ingredients and mix everything until smooth.

Tip: You can add lime zest to the top to give it a citrusy flavor or a few blueberries. You can even mix in some sunflower or sesame seeds to get it an additional crunch. Mixing it with finely chopped mint leaves adds a wonderfully fresh, minty flavor.

Image credit: Larisa Blinova

Keto Brownie

It's common to think that food items with flour all totally off the keto diet menu. However, there are plenty of alternatives out there nowadays as these flourless, keto-friendly brownies show. They are perfect for when you have a chocolate craving that cannot be curbed and best of all, they are low in carbs with the right amount of fat to keep you in a fat-burning state. These are also a great gluten-free dessert for those cutting out gluten or have an intolerance.

In this recipe, the ingredients yield 16 chocolate brownies. Each brownie contains 3 grams of carbohydrates.

Ingredients:

- 140 grams of milk chocolate (get the low-carb version that you can find at health stores. Also look out for diabetic chocolate which is sugar-free and made with sweeteners).
- 4 tablespoons of butter.
- 3 eggs.
- 170 grams of stevia sweetener.
- 85 grams of mascarpone cheese.
- 85 grams of cocoa powder (the darker, the better and always get unsweetened).
- A pinch of salt.

Method:

1 – Melt the chocolate in a bowl. Then add the butter and put the mix in the microwave for about 10 seconds. Stir it, and repeat this process until it is smooth. Leave to cool.

2 – In a different bowl, mix the three eggs and the sweetener until the mixture is frothy.

3 – Add in the mascarpone cheese, half of the cocoa powder, and the salt. Mix gently.

4 – Sift in the rest of the cocoa powder, stirring gently.

5 – Take the melted chocolate from step one (melt it again if it is not dissolved still) and slowly add that into the mix. It should be creamy with no lumps.

6 – Pour the mixture into a baking tray and bake for about 30 minutes. You will know when it is ready when the center of the mix is firm.

7 – Once cooked, leave it to cool down, then take it out of the pan and cut into squares.

Tip: Although these are low in carbs, they should be eaten sparingly on the keto diet as a treat as they are still high in calories and eating them regularly could impact your weight loss goals. However, once a week is perfectly fine. If you want to add some fruit to the mix, such as berries or pecan nuts, you can do that to give it some extra flavour.

Image credit: Martin Gardeazabel

Pecan Chocolate

This easy to make candy is perfect for a dinner party or just as a little something to satisfy a sweet tooth. The additional pecans give the dessert some extra nutrients and help keep it a low-carb and higher fat content sweet. Limit the amount you eat to keep the calories down, but a few will not put you off track with your keto diet.

This recipe makes 15 servings.
Each serving contains 3 grams of carbohydrates.

Ingredients:

- 115 grams of dark chocolate. Try getting a cocoa content of over 80%.
- 1 tablespoon of licorice powder.
- ½ teaspoon of liquid vanilla extract.
- 20 grams of chopped pecans.

Method:

1 – Melt the chocolate in the microwave. Once it is entirely melted, mix in the licorice powder and the vanilla extract. It should be liquid but still have a firm consistency.

2 – Line some parchment paper on a tray and pour over the chocolate mix. Sprinkle the pecans on top and let it cool by popping it in the fridge. Once it's set, crack the chocolate into pieces.

Image credit: Evmefoto

Coconut Cream Pie

Whenever you get those feelings for a coconut cream pie, these are a perfect choice. With a high-fat content (over 50 grams a serving) yet a low carb content, they fit in well with the keto diet. Remember to keep these as a treat for now and again and not something to eat every day. They maybe keto-friendly but they are still high in calories so should be eaten in moderation.

This recipe serves four people.
Each serving has 7 grams of carbohydrates.

Ingredients:
The ingredients are divided into three parts:

The crust of the pie:
- 4 tablespoons of butter (full-fat, unsalted).
- ¼ cup of sweetener. Erythritol is fine.
- 170 grams of almond flour.
- ¼ coconut flakes (unsweetened).

The custard part:
- 340 grams of thick whipping cream.
- 2 egg yolks.
- ¼ cup of coconut flour.
- ½ cup of water.
- 1 teaspoon of vanilla extract (you can use vanilla pods or liquid, whatever you have at home).
- ¼ of a cup of erythritol.

The top of the pie:
- 3 tablespoons of toasted coconut flakes.
- 170 grams of whipping cream.
- 15 drops of stevia sweetener.
- 1 teaspoon of vanilla extract.

Method:

1 – Start with the crust. Melt the butter in a pan and add the sweetener until it has dissolved. Then, mix in the almond flour and coconut flakes until everything is joining together. This will be the crust.

2 – Take the crust and spoon it into a pot or a ramekin. Allow it to cool.

3 – Now make the custard. Heat up the cream in a pot.

4 – Crack and separate the eggs separately and put the egg yolks in a different bowl.

5 – Mix the coconut flour and the water into the egg yolks.

6 – Stir in the vanilla into the cream that is heating up before adding the egg and coconut mix.

7 – Mix a lot until everything begins to thicken. Once it's thick, let it cool and then put on top of the crust in the ramekins. Leave inside the fridge for about an hour.

8 – Then, heat the coconut flakes until they begin to toast.

9 – In another bowl, mix the cream, the sweetener, and the vanilla. Beat until it forms peaks.

10 – Take the ramekins out of the fridge and spoon the cream on top of the custard. Then sprinkle with the toasted coconut flakes.

Image credit: Africa Studio

Banana Waffles

These low carb banana waffles can be a sweet treat for after dinner, or even used as a breakfast meal. The bananas are great for either a post or pre-workout snacks so you can eat these waffles before or after training to keep your energy levels high.

This recipe makes eight servings.
One serving contains 7 grams of carbohydrates.

Ingredients:

- 2 big, ripe bananas.
- 4 eggs.
- 250 grams of almond flour.
- 250 grams of coconut milk.
- A pinch of salt
- 1 teaspoon of baking powder.
- 1 teaspoon of vanilla extract.
- 1 teaspoon of cinnamon
- 1 tablespoon of ground psyllium husk powder.
- Coconut oil

Method:

1 – Take all the ingredients and put in a blender. Whizz it up and let it settle after.

2 – Spray a waffle maker with some coconut oil and pour in the mixture. Cook until a lovely golden brown.

3 – To serve, use whipped coconut cream or just a dollop of fresh, full-fat butter.

Image credit: Family Business

Low Carb Trifle

This trifle is a delicious low carb alternative to a regular trifle. Using avocado and coconut cream, the flavor has a tropical aftertaste and a rich, creamy texture. Serve with some raspberries or pecans to give it extra taste.

This recipe makes enough for four servings.
Each serving contains 8 grams of carbohydrates.

Ingredients:

- 1 avocado.
- 1 small banana.
- 250 grams of coconut cream.
- A squeeze of lime juice and the lime zest.
- 85 grams of raspberries.
- 55 grams of roasted pecans or walnuts.

Method:

1 – Mix the banana, the coconut cream, the avocado, and the lime juice and zest. Put the raspberries in a separate bowl and squeeze over the lime juice.

2 – Get a dessert bowl and make layers using the two mixtures. When you've used all the mixtures, top with some extra raspberries and a few roasted pecans.

Tip: For a festive trifle, add some cranberries instead of raspberries. You can also sprinkle it with cinnamon instead of pecans.

Image credit: Anna Shepulova

Yogurt Popsicles

A mix of berries and yogurt, these yogurt popsicles are perfect for those wanting something refreshing on a hot summer day. With just 5 grams of carbs per popsicle, they have at least half of the carb content of a regular ice cream making it a much better keto choice. They also have no added sugar and a higher fat and protein content, keeping you fuller for longer.

This recipe makes 12 popsicles.
Each popsicle contains 5 grams of carbohydrates.

Ingredients:

- 225 grams of chopped up mango that is frozen.
- 225 grams of halved strawberries, frozen.
- 1 cup of Greek yogurt. Get the full-fat version and as natural as possible.
- 8 tablespoons of full-fat cream.
- 1 teaspoon of vanilla extract.

Method:

1 – Let the mango and the strawberries defrost a little before putting them in the blender with the rest of the ingredients until everything is all smooth.

2 – Pour the mixture into popsicle molds and let them freeze for a few hours.

Tip: You can change the fruit to whatever you like, although avoid banana due to their high carb content. Orange with a squeeze of lime juice makes a acidy, refreshing popsicle flavor.

Image credit: Pada Smith

Berries And Whipped Cream

When you fancy a quick and simple dessert, this is by far one of the easiest to make. It's just sweetened cream served with berries. Although like most other desserts, it shouldn't regularly be eaten if you are watching your weight. It makes a great low-carb treat that is still high enough in fat to keep you full for a while.

This recipe serves two people.
Each serving has 6 grams of carbohydrates.

Ingredients:

- 250 grams of full-fat whipping cream.
- 1 cup or a handful of berries such as blueberries or strawberries. The best fruit you can use though is raspberries as they have a lower carb content than the other berries.
- 15 drops of stevia liquid sweetener.

Methods:

1 – You can use either fresh or frozen berries in this recipe. If they are frozen, let them defrost before using them.

2 – Put the cream into a bowl and whip it until smooth and peaks form. Halfway through whipping it, add the drops of sweetener.

3 – Sprinkle the berries on top of the cream and serve. Add some chopped mint for an extra dimension of flavor.

Image credit: Art nick

Chapter Summary:

In this chapter, we looked at ten delicious dessert recipes that are ideal for the keto diet.

- There is always a keto-friendly dessert available that doesn't fill you with carbs and uses alternative ingredients such as avocados, sweeteners, and fruits.

- Although these desserts are low in carb, they are still high in calories. As a result, they should be eaten sparingly and not consumed on a regular basis. However, when you fancy something sweet, or there is a special occasion, these treats are perfect.

In the next chapter, we will look at some great keto snacks that you can eat at home or take with you and eat in between meals during your daily activities.

Chapter Five: Keto Inspired Snacks

In this chapter, we will look at some great keto-friendly snacks.

If you spend a lot of your time outside of the home during the day, it can be hard finding keto-friendly snacks in local supermarkets and convenience stores. Not only may package-bought food have hidden sugar or additives, but it's also much harder to calculate how many carbs and fats there are in specific food items.

Therefore, it is a great idea to prepare your food in advance when on the keto diet. If you have free time on a sunday evening, for example, you can prepare your breakfasts, lunches, and dinners for the week ahead. It means that no matter how busy you get, you always have a keto-meal ready, so you are not tempted to just quickly order takeaway and derail from the tracks when it comes down to following a keto diet. The same rule applies to snacks. It's best to make some snacks in advance so you can take them out with you when you are out going about your daily activities. It makes sticking to your keto diet far easier, keeps you in a state of ketosis, and, most importantly, leaves you feeling satisfied, content, and not hungry.

So, when is the best time to eat snacks? The idea of a snack is to give us that little energy boost in between meals. It's not recommended to snack all throughout the day as it becomes hard to monitor your calorie intake and this can lead to you not achieving your weight loss goals. Your daily consumption of food should follow this pattern. First, you eat breakfast in the morning. Some people like to start the day with just a coffee then have breakfast a little bit later. Some prefer having breakfast straight away with a coffee or other preferred beverage. Either way is fine. After breakfast, your next meal will be lunch. In between these two meals, you should eat one snack if necessary. After lunch, your next meal will be dinner. In between these two meals, you can eat one snack again if you need it. After dinner, it's best to avoid snacking altogether, but if you still feel hungry, then a small high fat and high protein snack before bed is totally fine. Other than that, the rest of the day should be just drinking water. This habit will help you lose weight and stay on top of what you are eating.

How about snacks for working out? If you work out regularly, then you can include an extra couple of snacks. It is good to have a higher carb snack before you work out to give you plenty of energy and then a high-fat, moderate protein snack afterward. This is because the protein helps your muscles to grow and after a workout, your metabolism is at its highest so feeding it fat will help burn that and stored fat much quicker.

So, on the days you don't work out, follow the plan of having two or three snacks per day tops. If you do work out, you can have four or five snacks that day.

The following snacks are quick and easy to make and can be kept for a few days. You just need to pop them into a container and make sure you have some in your bag with you wherever you go.

In this chapter, we will look at the following snacks (in order):

- Cheese chips.
- Halloumi cheese wrapped in bacon.
- Cheese and cauliflower dip.
- Devilled eggs.
- Spicy roasted nuts.
- Seed Crackers.
- Garlic bread.
- Zucchini Nacho chips.
- Eggplant Fries.
- Kale chips

Cheese Chips

These cheese chips are high in fat and low in carbs and, best of all, super easy to make. They make an ideal snack at home served with guacamole or a simple, light snack while you're on-the-go. The cheese will help you stay fuller for longer too so you can make it to your next meal without feeling fatigue or lack of energy associated with hunger.

This recipe serves four people.
Each serving contains 2 grams of carbohydrates.

Ingredients:

- 225 grams of grated cheese (cheddar is great, or provolone).
- ½ teaspoon of paprika (in powder).

Method:

1 – Mould the grated cheese together in your hands and make little circles from it. Place them on a non-stick baking tray.

2 – Sprinkle with paprika. Then cook for about 8 minutes. If you notice they are starting to get golden brown quicker, reduce the heat and take them out sooner.

3 – Leave them to cool. And that's it!

Tip: Stick a wet, wooden lollipop stick in the middle of the cheese, so it melts around the stick. Make sure there is enough cheese either side by making one circle and laying it down on the tray, put the lollipop stick on top and then cover it with another cheese circle. They make a great snack for when you have guests around. You can also switch paprika for basil, thyme, or rosemary for different flavors.

Image credit: Iryna Imago

Halloumi Cheese Wrapped In Bacon

These snacks are irresistible and make a filling bite to eat in between meals. You can even add extra salad and sliced avocado to create a light yet satisfying lunch. Eat with a sour cream dip at home or take with you when you are out. The cheese will keep you full for a while, and the bacon increases the fat content to keep your fat-burning enzymes ticking over. They are also quick and easy to make.

This recipe makes 10 pieces of halloumi cheese.
Each serving has 3 grams of carbohydrates.

Ingredients:

- 225 grams of halloumi cheese.
- 150 grams of bacon.

Method:

1 – Cut the cheese into about 8 or 10 pieces.

2 – Take a slice of bacon and wrap one slice around each piece of cheese.

3 – Put on the baking tray and bake in the oven. It should take about 10 or 15 minutes, and the cheese and the bacon should be golden brown.

4 – Serve with some chopped chives if you like (optional).

Image credit: Elena Shashkina

Cheese And Cauliflower Dip

This snack is an idea for the whole family, and although it is keto -friendly, it is also a delicious snack for those that are not on the keto diet. Instead of the processed, carb-loaded cheese dips that are bought from the stores and often contain high levels of sugars, why not try this cheese and cauliflower dip that is high in fat and low in sugar and carbs. It's perfect as a dip with sliced carrots, cucumber, celery, or any other low-carb vegetable.

This recipe serves about 20 servings.
Each serving contains just over 1 gram of carbohydrates.

Ingredients:

- 450 grams of cauliflower.
- 500 ml of chicken broth (if you can make it, great! If not, just make sure to read the labels of the shop-bought ones).
- ½ an onion, diced.
- 85 grams of mayonnaise.
- 255 grams of cream cheese.
- ½ teaspoon of cumin.
- ½ teaspoon of chili powder.
- ½ teaspoon garlic powder.
- ½ teaspoon pepper.
- Salt to taste.

Method:

1 – Cook the cauliflower with the onion in the chicken broth. Wait until it's soft and then add the cumin, garlic powder, the chili powder, the salt, and the pepper.

2 – Add in the cream cheese and mix with the cauliflower until

smooth.

3 – Use a hand blender to blend everything again and make sure it is extra smooth.

4 – Add the mayonnaise and gently whisk that in.

5 – Chill in the fridge for about 3 hours. Then it's ready to serve with fresh vegetable sticks.

Image credit: Dagmar Breu

Devilled Eggs

Eggs aren't just for breakfast and can, in fact, make excellent snacks. Eggs are rich in fats and a source of protein too, a combination that helps keep us full for longer. These devilled eggs are best made and consumed on the same day as they don't last very long. It's one of those treats for a day where you have some time you can spare and feel like cooking something different. These devilled eggs come with a slight twist as they use cream cheese instead of mayonnaise.

This recipe serves four people.
Each serving contains 6 grams of carbohydrates.

Ingredients:

- 6 eggs (for this recipe, the larger, the better).
- 1 and ¼ cup of water.
- ½ a cup of soy sauce (or about 185 ml).
- ¼ cup of rice vinegar (or 90 ml).
- 1 teaspoon of stevia liquid sweetener.
- 2 cloves of garlic (mince them in the garlic crusher).
- 115 grams of cream cheese.
- 1 tablespoon of fresh chives finely chopped.
- Salt and pepper to taste.

Method:

1 – Boil the eggs until firm.

2 – Mix one cup of water, half a cup of soy sauce, a quarter of a cup of rice vinegar, a teaspoon of stevia, and the crushed garlic cloves all together in a bowl.

3 – Peel the eggs and put them in the marinade in step two. Here comes the clever part: lay paper towels over the tops of the eggs, allowing the sides of the towels to touch the marinade. The paper will then absorb the marinade and cover the tops of the eggs with the marinade, so everything gets equally covered.

4 – Leave the eggs in the fridge for about 2 hours, turning every now and again to make sure it's all covered evenly.

5 - Then, take the eggs out, cut in half, and remove the yolks.

6 – Mix the cream cheese in a separate bowl with ¼ cup of water. You may find you need less. Then mix in the chopped chives and the egg yolks as well as a little bit of salt and pepper.

7 – Get the yolk and cream cheese mix and spoon it into the egg whites. To serve, sprinkle more chives, some paprika and dill, or some pepper on the top.

Image credit: Brent Hofacker

Spicy Roasted Nuts

The wonderful thing about these nuts as a snack is you know exactly what is in them so you can be sure that they have no hidden sugars or any extra additives. Nuts are a popular keto snack as they are high in fat and some are low in carbs (avoid cashew and pistachio those are very high in carbs). You can make these nuts in advance and save them for a long time. Put them in a container and take them out with you when you leave the house to eat as a healthy, keto snack.

This recipe serves six people.
Each serving contains 2 grams of carbohydrates.

Ingredients:

- 230 grams of nuts (pecans, walnuts, or almonds are perfect).
- 1 teaspoon of salt.
- 1 tablespoon of olive oil (or you can even use coconut oil).
- 1 teaspoon of ground cumin.
- 1 teaspoon of paprika powder (or chili powder if you prefer).

Method:

1 – Mix the ingredients in a frying pan at a medium temperature. Make sure the nuts are warmed up and not burnt.

2 – Mix well, take off the heat and let them cool.

Tip: You can use pumpkin spice to give the nuts a bit of seasonal taste or cinnamon as well. Another option is to replace the cumin and paprika with thyme and rosemary for a strong herb flavor.

Image credit: Sibirianblueberry

Seed Crackers

These delicious seed crackers are easy to make and easy to take on the go. Low in carbs and high in fat, they make a great snack for when you feel peckish before your next meal. Although it is suggested here as a stand-alone snack, it also makes a great addition to a cheese board or a side to breakfast, lunch, or dinner dishes.

This recipe makes 15 crackers.
Each serving (per cracker) is 1 gram of carbohydrates.

Ingredients:

- 3 tablespoons of almond flour
- 3 tablespoons of sunflower seeds.
- 3 tablespoons of pumpkin seeds.
- 3 tablespoons of chia seeds.
- 3 tablespoons of sesame seeds.
- ½ tablespoon of ground psyllium husk powder.
- ½ tablespoon coconut oil.
- ½ cup of boiling hot water.
- Pinch of salt.

Method:

1 – Mix all the dry ingredients before adding the water and the oil, mixing carefully.

2 – The ingredients will form a type of dough. Spread out on a baking tray and bake for about 45 minutes. Turn the oven off and let the crackers dry inside.
3 – Once cool, break into pieces before spreading plenty of butter on top.

Tip: Want to make the crackers nut free? Then simply switch the almond flour for sesame seed flour.

Image credit: id-art

Garlic Bread

Who would have guessed that, you can even have garlic bread that tastes like the real deal, yet is very low in carbs at just one gram per serving. Eat these as a snack or as a side dish to a meal when you want something a little more substantial.

This recipe makes five servings.
A serving has 1 gram of carbohydrates.

Ingredients:

For the bread:
- 5 tablespoons of almond flour.
- ½ teaspoon of baking powder.
- ¼ teaspoon of salt.
- 1 and ¼ tablespoons of ground psyllium husk powder.
- ½ teaspoon of white wine vinegar (or it can be cider vinegar).
- 5 tablespoons of boiling water.
- 1 egg white.

For the garlic butter:
- 30 grams of butter (full-fat).
- 1 garlic clove, minced up or chopped very finely.
- ½ tablespoon of finely chopped parsley.
- A pinch of salt.

Method:

1 – Mix all the dry ingredients.

2 – Add the vinegar, the egg white, and the boiled water to the bowl and mix thoroughly until it's like a dough.

3 – Roll out five pieces into hot dog shapes. Put on the baking tray.

Tip: The bread will almost double in size so leave plenty of room.

4 – Cook for about 45 minutes.

5 – While the bread is cooking, make the garlic butter by mixing the butter, the garlic, the parsley, and a pinch of salt.

6 – When the bread is ready, take it out of the oven and spread the garlic butter on top. Bake for another 10 minutes until golden brown.

Tip: Serve with a layer of grated cheese on top for cheesy garlic bread. Use parmesan or another type of hard cheese to keep the fat content up and the carb levels down.

Image credit: Chachamp

Zucchini Nacho Chips

The perfect snack for when you are craving crisps or need a nacho substitute, these zucchini nacho chips are low carb and packed with flavor. Eat at home with salsa or sour cream, or simply take with you when you are out as a healthy, keto-friendly snack.

This recipe serves 4 people.
Each serving contains 2 grams of carbohydrates.

Ingredients:

- 1 zucchini.
- 500 grams of coconut oil.
- Salt to taste.
- A sprinkle of tex-mex seasoning.

Method:

1 – Cut the zucchini into very thin slices and sprinkle with plenty of salt.

2 – Heat up a pan of oil and cook the zucchini slices at a high temperature.
3 – Once the slices begin to turn golden brown, they are ready to be taken out of the pan. Put them on a paper towel to get rid of the excess oil.
4 - Sprinkle with the tex-mex seasoning and they are ready to be eaten.

Tip: You can use other seasonings too. Experiment with thyme, rosemary, or sprinklings of sesame seeds for an extra crunch.

Image credit: Nancykasz

Eggplant Fries

Craving chips? Then these eggplant fries offer the perfect substitute. They make a great snack to be eaten just by themselves or with a pot of homemade mayonnaise. Alternatively, they can be used as a side for your lunch or dinner. The almond flour gives them a few carbs so they will make an excellent pre-workout snack to boost your energy levels up for your training session. The great thing about these fries is that you can make a large batch and freeze them for future use.

This recipe makes eight servings.
Each serving contains 5 grams of carbohydrates.

Ingredients:

- 2 eggplants.
- 700 grams of almond flour.
- 1 tablespoon of cayenne pepper.
- Salt and pepper to taste.
- 2 eggs.
- Coconut oil.

Method:

1 – Cut the eggplant into French-fries or into wedges, whichever you prefer.
2 – Mix the almond flour, the salt, the pepper, and the cayenne pepper. Whisk the egg in a different bowl.
3 – Take a piece of eggplant and dip it into the egg. Then dip it into the flour mixture making sure it's entirely covered. Then dip it back into the egg and a final dip into the flour.
4 – Put the eggplant pieces on a baking tray once they are covered entirely and drizzle the coconut oil over the top. Then bake for about

15 minutes. They will look a bit crispy and have a nice golden-brown color once they are ready.

Image credit: teleginatania

Kale Chips

This simple snack can be made in batches and well in advance, so you have snacks to take out with you wherever you go. Kale is very low in carbs, so it's an ideal snack for those on the keto diet. At home, you can eat it with sour cream or crème fraiche for a fulfilling and tasty snack.

This recipe makes four servings.
Each serving contains 3 grams of carbohydrates.

Ingredients:

- 200 grams of kale.
- Salt.
- Olive oil.
- White wine vinegar.

Method:

1 – Tear the leaves of the kale into rough, small pieces. Then mix with olive oil and the white wine vinegar.
2 – Sprinkle the leaves with salt.
3 – Put the kale on a baking tray and cook for about 15 minutes. The leaves should become crispy. Take them out of the oven if they look crispy before 15 minutes as you don't want to burn them. Serve with a sprinkle of sea salt.

Tip: Add a sprinkle of grated parmesan cheese for some cheesy kale crisps.

Image credit: Brent Hofacker

Chapter Summary:

In this chapter, we saw ten healthy snacks that you can eat in between meals on the keto diet. You can also use these as sides for your main courses.

- These snacks are easy to do and to be taken out with you when you are not at home.

- There are also snacks that provide alternatives for classic favorites such as chips and crisps, yet the keto versions are much healthier and will keep you on track with your diet.

In the next chapter, we will look at some keto-friendly drinks.

Chapter Six: Drinks For The Keto Diet

In this chapter, we will look at drinks you can have that are keto-friendly and will give you a break from drinking water.

Although by far the best drink you can have on the keto diet is water, sometimes it's refreshing to have a change. One great idea you can try is to add different flavors to water. Fill up a large bottle with water and add some thyme and some ginger to give a tasty alternative to just plain water. Also, you can add a squeeze of lime, lemon, or orange to give your water a citrus flavor.

When you fancy something a bit different though, here are some alternative drinks you can have now and again on the keto diet. One of the most commonly asked questions for people starting the keto diet is if they can drink alcohol. Ideally, it is best to avoid alcohol. Beer is out, although some special beers have fewer carbs and you can get away with one or two sometimes. Unsweetened white wine is allowed if you just have a glass occasionally. Drinks such as vodka, rum, and brandy don't have any carbs so are ok to drink from ketogenic perspective, of course drink in moderation as alcohol is not a healthy substance to any diet if consumed excessively. Avoid cocktails at all cost as they are incredibly high in calories.

You can liven up vodka by mixing it with freshly squeezed lime juice, add 10 drops (or more) of stevia liquid sweetener and serve with plenty of ice. If you are at a social gathering and want to drink along with everyone else, this is a great drink to order.

Note: try to stick to water and drink at least eight glasses per day. However, occasionally, these low-carb drinks are ok to have as a treat.

411

In this chapter, we will look at the following drink recipes (in order):

- ☐ Blueberry smoothie

- ☐ Iced Tea

- ☐ Bulletproof Coffee

- ☐ Eggnog

- ☐ Dairy-free Latte

Blueberry Smoothie

This smoothie is a great drink for the afternoon and is so full of nutrients that it can even be a stand-alone snack or a breakfast option. It is low carb and delicious and is also a great pre-workout snack to get some extra energy before training. This recipe is with blueberries, but you can change it to strawberries or blackberries if you prefer.

This recipe serves two people.

One serving contains 11 grams of carbohydrates. (so, it is a low carb drink yet still higher in carbs than others, so drink in moderation).

Ingredients:

- 400 grams of coconut milk.
- 170 grams of blueberries. Frozen is just as good as fresh.
- A squeeze of lemon juice.
- ½ teaspoon of liquid vanilla extract.

Method:

1 – Simply put all the ingredients into a blender and whizz it up until smooth.

2 -Pour over some ice for a refreshing smoothie. Serve with a sprig of mint on the top.

Image credit: Africa Studio

Iced Tea

This incredibly refreshing drink is perfect for a hot summer day when you need to feel refreshed. Thirst-quenching and delicious, it doesn't contain any carbs so you can drink it as much as you like. It makes a great addition to a dinner party when served in a large jug.

This recipe serves two people.
Each serving contains 0 carbohydrates.

Ingredients:

- 2 cups of cold water.
- 1 cup of ice cubes.
- 1 or 2 tea bags (your favorite flavor).
- Other additional flavorings such as sliced lemons, ginger, fresh mint, or sprigs of thyme.

Method:

1 – Mix the cold water in a jug with the tea and the flavoring of your choice. Then leave it in the fridge for about 2 hours.

2 – Take the tea bag out and leave the flavouring in to keep the water constantly infused.

3 – Add the ice cubes to a couple of glasses and pour in the mixture.

Tip: You can use any tea bag you like, and you can make much bigger quantities to serve more people. Try fruits like a peach as well which leaves behind a soft, fruity, summery flavor.

Image credit: Africa Studio.

Bulletproof Coffee

This is quite a famous coffee in the keto world. It has zero carbohydrates and yet a high-fat content, making it a great start to the day to kick start those fat-burning enzymes. It is also good if you are about to work out and don't have time for a snack. Drinking this coffee will give you energy and stimulation to power through your workout with no problem.

This recipe makes one serving.
Each serving contains 0 grams of carbohydrates.

Ingredients:

- 1 cup of hot coffee. Brew it just before you will make this to keep the coffee fresh.
- 1 tablespoon of coconut oil.
- 1 tablespoon of full-fat butter (use unsalted)/

Method:

1 – Mix all the ingredients until it's smooth. Then drink while it's hot. If you like your coffee extra sweet, add some drops of stevia liquid sweetener.

Image credit: SewCream

Eggnog

Typically, alcohol is not offered on the keto menu as it contains elevated levels of carbs and often leads to unhealthy food choices. However, some alcohol you can drink especially in small doses such as rum, vodka, or brandy, as long as they are unsweetened. As keto is a lifestyle, it is essential to have some flexibility, and this eggnog lets you drink when the party season arrives. With just 5 grams of carbohydrates per serving, it is good for the keto diet. However, it is still high in calories so limit your intake to just one, maximum two if you want to keep on track with your weight loss goals.

This recipe serves four people.
Each serving contains 5 grams of carbohydrates.

Ingredients:

- 2 egg yolks.
- 1 orange – you want its juice and its zest.
- 4 tablespoons of dark liquor. You can use rum or brandy, for example.
- 1 cup of full-fat cream.
- ½ a teaspoon of honey.
- ½ a teaspoon of vanilla (pod or liquid extract).
- A pinch of ground nutmeg.

Method:

1 – Mix the yolks, the vanilla extract, and the honey together. Whisk until it is smooth.

2 – Add a squeeze of orange juice and some orange zest. Then add the liquor, mixing well.

3 – Whisk the cream up and then add it to the egg mix.

4 – Pour the mix into glasses and let it settle a little to allow it to marinate.

5 – Sprinkle some nutmeg and cinnamon on top and serve.

Image credit: Anna Shepulova

Dairy Free Latte

This latte is a perfect coffee for the morning, especially for those that are cutting out dairy from their diets. It's also quick and easy to make, and with just 1 gram of carbohydrates, it provides a great start to the day. If you don't fancy eating breakfast yet still want some energy, drink this latte with whipped coconut cream on top. This will boost energy levels as well as increase the fat content.

This recipe contains ingredients for two servings.
Each serving contains 1 gram of carbohydrates.

Ingredients:

- 2 eggs (organic if possible).
- A large cup of boiling water.
- A few drops of vanilla extract.
- 2 tablespoons of coconut oil.
- Optional: a sprinkle of ground ginger or cinnamon.

Method:

1 – Mix all the ingredients together in blender. Serve straight away.

Image credit: Jack Jelly

Chapter Summary:

In this chapter, we saw several drinks that you can have which are considered fine to drink on the keto diet.

- Whenever possible, try drinking water as it is the best drink for your body and doesn't contain any carbs or calories. However, sometimes a break from water is desired, and if that's the case, then these drinks are a great alternative to be had every once in awhile

- Bear in mind that even though these drinks are low in carbs, many still have high levels of calories so make sure to drink in moderation.

- The keto eggnog provides a seasonal, alcoholic drink that you can have while still sticking to the keto guidelines of low carbs and high-fat content.

Final Words

You have reached the end of *"The Complete Ketogenic Cookbook."* Thanks for sticking with me right to the end.

I wrote this book to combine my experience and knowledge of making delicious, simple, yet keto-friendly meals. I hope I managed to produce at least some recipes that you liked and have inspired you to continue searching for new low-carb meals. There are plenty out there. It just takes a little creativity and imagination.

An excellent idea is to make a copy of the recipes from this book that you liked the most and start building up your own collection of all the keto recipes that you enjoy. This will give you a bounty of delicious meal options that will help you stick to the keto diet and make the most of this healthy lifestyle.

These recipes will help you keep your carb count low and help you continue to have a healthy, keto lifestyle that will not only make you look great but feel fantastic too.

Good luck with keto cooking and enjoy the journey of discovering new foods.

Made in the USA
San Bernardino, CA
29 June 2018